HAPPY HOUR

in the

HIGH PEAKS

To Grampa, who loved a roaring campfire and a cold Genny; to Gram, whose nightly highball inspired our recipes; and to Cosimo. Your manhattans will be missed.

To our loving husbands, Tony & Bob, and our families, who came to equate Happy Hour with take-out. We thank them for standing by us while we visited bars and mixed up innumerable drink recipes in the name of "research."

And to Sydney, who constantly reminded us that what we were doing was "stupid" and that no one would buy our book.

HAPPY HOUR

in the

HIGH PEAKS

An Adirondack Bar Guide

——————————— by Kim Ladd & Pam Ladd ———————————

Library of Congress Control Number: 2013939000

ISBN-13: 978-1-939216-08-3
ISBN-10: 1-939216-08-7

Visit us at
www.happyhourinthehighpeaks.com

Produced by
Bloated Toe Publishing, Peru, NY 12972

Printed and bound by
Versa Press, 1465 Spring Bay Road, East Peoria, IL 61611-9788

Manufactured in the United States of America

Contents

Introduction

What happens when you combine a simple question between two sisters and a 900-mile car ride? Why, *Happy Hour in the High Peaks*, of course. Pam wondered if a drink she had created, the Adirondack Mudslide, would appear on a web search. Kim consulted her smart-phone. It did not. So, how do we get it there? We decided we would have to write a blog about drink recipes, and we started brainstorming. After all, we had 14 hours to kill. Each way. We turned up the music to drown out the eye rolling from our daughters in the back seat.

Somewhere in Virginia, the subject of writing an Adirondack-themed bar book came into the conversation. We first thought about a cocktail recipe book. A bar guide. There are already thousands of bar guides out there, so we had to find some way to make it unique. We looked at each other and both said, at the same time, "A *bar* guide!" We knew what we meant. A guide to the bars, as well as a cocktail bar guide. Our teachers always told us to write what we know. We know more than a little bit about bars, booze, and beer—enough to write about them anyway. We were on a roll and hatched this fun and crazy notion that we would visit as many bars as possible, the only rule being that they would all have to be inside the Blue Line.

Pam suggested the 46er idea—visit all of the bars, select our favorite 46, and write a detailed review of each one. There are 46 High Peaks in the Adirondack Mountains. Our High Peaks are bars, taverns, and inns with elevations that measure above average, show promise of longevity, offer diversity, and are venues that anyone would find comfortable. In January 2011, we struck out on an adventure to review all of the bars in the Adirondack Park. Our husbands just shook their heads.

We visited over 120 bars inside the Blue Line. In making our selections, sometimes 46 felt like too many and sometimes not enough. Many required debate or a repeat visit. Those that were hard to cut from the High Peaks are listed here as Trailheads—worthy of a visit if you're in the neighborhood. We are frequently asked what our favorite bars are, but there are so many—46 to be exact.

The Adirondack Park is 9,375 square miles, or 6.1 million acres. We covered it. Given the size of the park, we decided to break it into five regions: Foothills, Eastern Lakes, Southern & Sacandaga, High Peaks, and Western Wilderness. Our Adirondack bar guide contains reviews of 46 bars, a summary of their amenities at-a-glance, and a brief outline of the Trailheads, all listed by region. The recipe section features our own drink recipes, and signature drink recipes contributed by many of the High Peaks bars.

Our High Peaks aren't necessarily the jumping joints or the

hopping hotspots. They are pubs and bars where staff and owners care about their customers, and the patrons are not overtly territorial. From honky-tonk to high-end pub, each one offers something a little different. Some have been around for 100 years, while others are in their infancy. Atmosphere varies from place to place, from contemporary Adirondack-style decor to historic landmarks with sloping floors and layer upon layer of paint.

Like the Adirondack High Peaks, some are going to be a more difficult climb, depending on your fitness level. Be sure to read our piece, A Good Bar Attender, to limber up before your ascent. Like any Adirondack adventure, it's best to be prepared.

Know your trails. Refer to the High Peaks At-a-Glance table for facts about your destinations.

Know your limitations. Determine how many bars you will visit in a given time frame. You may need accommodations. Don't set out on the trail with an empty stomach. Keep energy levels high by eating when necessary. While it's important to stay hydrated, pace yourself, or enlist a designated driver.

Pack accordingly. Bring your Happy Hour bar guide and passport. *Happy Hour in the High Peaks* hats and t-shirts are helpful in identifying you as a 46er. A GPS is optional; asking for directions is risky. Cell phones can be helpful, but are often useless within the Adirondack Park.

The benefits of our escapade were far greater than we imagined. We got to know the Adirondacks more intimately, met interesting characters, and made new friends. Old friends gathered at Pammy's At-Her-on-Deck Pub, official drink lab and tasting facility, to critique and perfect specimens, happy to share their expertise while drinking free booze.

In order to share the experience, visit our High Peaks as a 46er with Happy Hour Passport in hand. Need a passport? The Happy Hour Passport, available on our website, is a coupon book with drink discounts at all of the High Peaks bars. Present the passport for stamped validation at each location. Use the bar guide to check out the High Peaks and Trailheads within the park. Use the drink guide to entertain at home or to order a signature drink on the Happy Hour Trail.

According to the *New York Times*, the Adirondacks is one of 46 "places to go" in 2013. Here are 46 more.

Cheers and Bottoms Up!
Kim & Pam

A Good Bar Attender

While most Adirondackers are not, by nature, predatory, they have been known to be territorial. Following some simple rules should help in acculturation.

1. Don't be an a$$#@!*. It will only raise hackles.

2. Be observant. Remember, you are an invasive species. When encroaching on an unfamiliar habitat, be considerate of the dominant life forms and prevailing climate. From biker bar to bistro, behavior will vary. The old adage "When in Rome …" applies here.

3. Smile (not to be confused with baring your teeth) and make eye contact with the bartender (usually the alpha) as quickly as possible. It's her job to be nice to you, so take advantage of that. Keep in mind, however, the bartender can quickly turn on you (see rule #1). Acceptance by indigenous residents is an important aspect of socialization among the multifarious visitors. Once you have the approval and trust of the bartender, as demonstrated to patrons through body language or otherwise, you'll be a member of the pack in no time!

4. If you've just walked into a tavern and feel compelled to turn and run, DON'T! They can smell fear. Just smile confidently, approach the bar, and order the strongest drink you can handle. It might turn out to be the best time you've had in the Adirondacks!

5. Not sure what you want to drink? Look for signs or a beverage menu listing drink specials, or ask your server for suggestions if he isn't too busy. If you need a few minutes, don't be afraid to tell the bartender, but do let him go while you decide. If it's obviously a beer joint, don't order a foofoo drink like a frozen daiquiri or a piña colada. You're likely to irritate the bartender and you won't be happy with his

rendition of the drink. If you're not a beer or wine drinker, keep your mixed drink within the established boundaries.

6. Make small talk with the nearest patron. Remember, they're just as afraid of you. If you're new in town, ask about a local landmark. Then *listen* to the response. If you're not interested in the topic, don't ask in the first place. At all times, avoid controversial topics like religion, politics, and even sports. If staff or patrons bring it up, smile and nod agreeably. Your two safest conversations are the weather and the *Happy Hour in the High Peaks* review of their tavern. The latter is likely to warrant a more interesting and lively conversation!

7. Keep your own small talk to a minimum. People love to talk about themselves. Let them. Don't monopolize, don't interrupt, and remember to listen. Again, when in doubt, see rule #1.

8. Be a good tipper. Leave your money on the bar, indicating to the server that all of this could be hers, if treated properly. An offering to the alpha will not go unnoticed by the pack.

9. Don't talk on your cell phone. It's a clear indication that the people around you aren't important enough for your attention, and it's like turning your back on the predator. If you must make or receive a call, take it outside. Once outside, give the smokers some distance. That is their sanctuary, so don't make them uncomfortable too. It is, however, perfectly acceptable to use your smartphone to look up *Happy Hour in the High Peaks* drink recipes and reviews.

10. Don't stay too long. The bartender and patrons have been waiting for a new topic of discussion, and *you* will most likely be it. They can't talk about you until you leave, so get going! Furthermore, the longer you stay, the more likely you are to break rule #1!

Whether you're alone or in a pack, discovering a new pub doesn't need to be a hair-raising experience. You can hunker down in low conversation, stealing furtive glances, earning mistrust and suspicion, or you can use your social instincts to meet new people and learn about them. The most important fact we have discovered in all our wanderings is that you get out of a place what you put into it.

The Adirondack Park

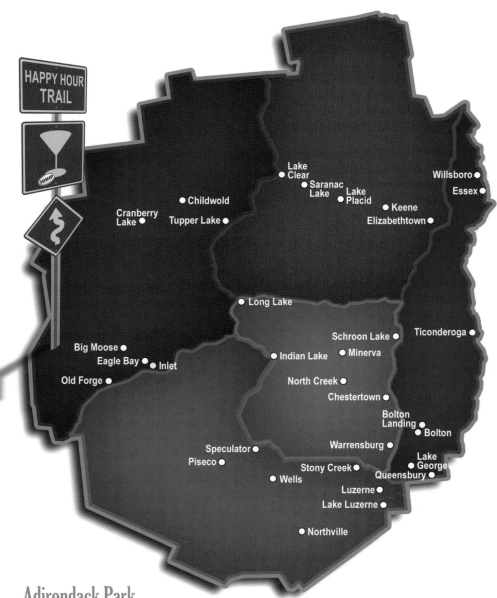

Adirondack Park

We have separated the Adirondack Park into five regions for the Happy Hour Tour. Although the Happy Hour Trail won't take you to every remote corner of the Park, we think it will provide a glimpse of the diverse people and places within.

The Regions

Foothills Region

The Foothills Region is the gateway to the Adirondack Park. From Warrensburg to Long Lake, this region is home to some of the oldest taverns in the Adirondacks. There's something for every season in the Foothills: summer camping or boating on the many lakes, autumn leaf peeping, winter skiing at Gore Mountain, and spring whitewater rafting on the Hudson River.

Eastern Lakes Region

The Eastern Lakes Region covers an area from Queensbury to Willsboro. Although 10 of the 11 Eastern Lakes taverns are open year-round, this region is best enjoyed in the summer. Discover some beautiful lake views along Route 9N.

Southern & Sacandaga Region

Great Sacandaga Lake is the focal point of this region, but the Luzerne area is popular for river rafting and horseback riding. Speculator, Wells, and Piseco have smaller but pristine lakes, and plenty of Adirondack history. The Southern & Sacandaga Region is as popular with snowmobilers as it is with boaters.

High Peaks Region

This is a mecca for extreme or adventure sports enthusiasts. Whether climbing the High Peaks, training for Olympic events, or visiting Saranac Lake for the annual soccer tournament, there's always adventure in the High Peaks. Each town in the region has something different to see and do.

Western Wilderness Region

From Cranberry Lake to Old Forge, this is one of the most remote regions in the Adirondack Park. Cranberry Lake is perfect for an authentic summer retreat. Southerly, Old Forge is a summer hotspot with attractions for everyone. During the winter, the whole region is a snowmobiler's paradise.

THE BLUE LINE

Foothills Region

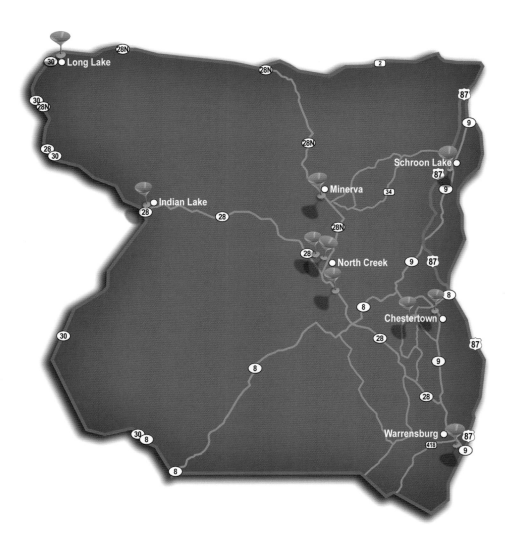

Region I: Foothills Division

The Bars

Chestertown
- 🍸 Friends Lake Inn Wine Bar
- 🍸 Panther Mountain Pub

Indian Lake
- 🍸 Indian Lake Restaurant & Tavern

Long Lake
- 🍸 Adirondack Hotel Tap Room

Minerva
- 🍸 Sporty's Iron Duke Saloon

North Creek
- 🍸 barVino
- 🍸 Basil & Wick's
- 🍸 Trapper's Tavern at Copperfield Inn

Schroon Lake
- 🍸 Witherbee's Carriage House

Warrensburg
- 🍸 George Henry's

FOOTHILLS

Adirondack Hotel Tap Room

Even if there weren't a gift shop lined with books of local interest, the Adirondack Hotel in Long Lake was an immediate contender as one of the 46 High Peaks bars in the Adirondacks. Grand and impressive, rustic and refined, the three-story structure with rough slab siding, gabled roof, and sprawling porches typical of century-old Adirondack inns is a commanding presence overlooking Long Lake.

The original hotel opened in 1879 as Kellogg's Lake House, which was later destroyed by fire. It was rebuilt and opened as the Adirondack Hotel in 1904. Surviving devastating fires and, most recently, the flood of 2011, the Adirondack Hotel still speaks of its original grandeur in a place where its history and its people endure.

The hotel entrance is guarded by wildlife of impressive proportions. A six-foot-tall black bear stares in silent greeting while a moose head oversees check-ins at the antique reception desk. Victorian antiques accent the light and airy sitting and dining rooms. Simple, two-bulb pendant chandeliers suspended from white painted tin ceilings cast their light on several Adirondack folk paintings, including two portraits of Noah John Rondeau, famous Adirondack hermit.

Step from the worn linoleum tiles to the aged wood floor of the Tap Room, tucked away in a far corner of the hotel, and feel the history of the bar at the Adirondack Hotel. Rustic and dim, the rough pine walls, polished bar, and dark barstools present contrast to the sunny lobby and dining areas. Peering from among three televisions, the taxidermied eyes of many animals look on, unseeing. Rumored to have once been a busy stop on the Underground Railroad, and a hub of anti-Prohibition commerce, the hotel contains secret passages and hidden rooms, all but forgotten now.

Offering a small but diverse microbrew selection, which varies seasonally, the Adirondack Hotel's signature drink is the draft lineup, featuring four craft and two domestic beers. Standard liquor and bottled beers are also available, at about average prices. Happy Hour

1245 Main Street, Route 30, Long Lake

518.624.4700

SUMMER HOURS:

Daily
Open at 11 am

OFF-SEASON HOURS:

Daily
Open at 11 am

CLOSED

Major holidays

is when you're there, but no special pricing applies.

A deck off the bar, overlooking the lake, has a variety of options for fair-weather seating. Although bar service is not offered outside, drinks are welcome on the deck and on the front porch. The front porch is furnished with dining tables and a row of red rockers from which to enjoy the fresh air and view of the lake and mountains. The Adirondack Hotel is open year-round. The Tap Room closes for Christmas, Easter, and Thanksgiving, but the hotel remains open. Entertainment is featured throughout the year in the form of open mic night and a variety of musical entertainers.

Carol and Carmine Inserra have owned the Adirondack Hotel for the past 21 years. Carol is a lovely and gracious woman with a relaxed and pleasant demeanor. Carmine handles most of the maintenance, but is known to take more interest in the chicken and ribs barbecue he hosts every Wednesday and Saturday all summer long. The hotel offers 18 rooms, an apartment, and a suite; some with private bath, and none with phone or television, though a TV can be found on each floor's common room. Cell service and open WiFi are available for those who want to stay connected.

The bar entertains locals all year and tourists in summer and winter, and lists Helen Keller, Jack Dempsey, Mick Jagger, Mickey Mantle, and maybe an author or two among its famous visitors. According to the Adirondack Hotel's website, "Before you leave, everyone will know your name." With pleasant, professional staff, and friendly, forthcoming locals, you'll want to linger as long as you can and wander freely inside and out.

adirondackhotel.com

barVino

O ne of three *Happy Hour in the High Peaks* favorite Adirondack bars in North Creek, barVino is testament to this community's tireless effort to grow, change, and appeal to the masses.

There's more to North Creek than outdoor recreation. Sure, Gore Mountain is the sun around which the region revolves, but there's a fresh new energy in town. Trendy downtown shops and eateries are comfortably situating themselves among ski rental shops, hardware store, and family market. The Tannery Pond Community Center, with its art gallery exhibits and theater performances, draws its own unique patronage.

Concealed amid the rusticity of North Creek, barVino is a refined and polished gem waiting to be unearthed. BarVino's unpretentious sophistication is a refreshing variation on the usual Adirondack theme. As the name implies, wine is the focus of this charming bistro, but the beer menu muscles its way in, vying for equal billing. A wine bar with a little bit of attitude.

A high tin ceiling, clean simple lines, and rich contrasting colors convey a sense of order complemented with a touch of whimsy. Works by area artists are regularly displayed on the walls. The concrete bar, built by owner Mike Bowers, is the focal point of the room, radiating warmth not ordinarily associated with concrete. A window behind the bar exhibits a glimpse of the adjacent wine cellar. Centered behind the bar, a wine refrigerator, built much like an apothecary's chest, stands ready for dispensing. Thought has gone into every detail, from the continually evolving menu to the ladies' room, where an eclectic collection of antique mirrors hangs in the hallway and a vintage oak dry sink holds baskets of fresh linens.

At least 30 wines are available by the glass, and the adjoining wine cellar offers additional inventory of nearly 100 choices by the bottle. The five-page wine list requires a passport—selections from Italy, Spain, France, Germany, Australia, New Zealand, Chile, and California in red, rose, port, white, dessert, and champagne. The beer menu lists nearly 50 varieties of lagers, ales, wheats, Belgians, stouts, porters, and a dozen craft drafts as well, from local to international. For those whose tastes are more accustomed to mass production, PBR lurks among its more worldly cousins. Pricing is surprisingly reasonable, average for the area. A glass of wine ranges from $5 to $16 for a five-ounce pour; bottled (and canned) beer from $2.75 to $18, though most are under $6.

BarVino classifies its menu as "rustic chic." A tapas menu, offering small plates of charcuterie, artisanal cheeses, salads, and other delectable morsels, changes often with the seasons and availability of local products. Instead of typical pub fare, expect to find such delicacies on the menu as Mediterranean olives, llama and ricotta meatballs, house-made duck rillettes, and pan-seared elk rack. The kitchen is open Tuesday through Saturday from 5 to 9 p.m., and Sunday from 4 to 8 p.m.

Patrons at barVino are a blend of local and part-time residents, vacationers, and visitors who come for the food and wine but stick around for the company or Wednesday night music, usually a jazz band. BarVino has been a family-run establishment since 2008. Mike, Anna, and Luke Bowers have managed to impart that feeling among their guests at barVino and try to have a family member on staff at all times.

North Creek continues to grow and change without sacrificing its identity. It is, in fact, forming one. Rivaling locations of greater notoriety like Lake Placid, barVino is just one of many reasons to visit North Creek, where local simplicity meets urban chic.

FOOTHILLS

518.251.0199

SUMMER HOURS:
Tuesday - Sunday
Open at 4 pm

OFF-SEASON HOURS:
Tuesday - Sunday
Open at 4 pm

CLOSED
Major holidays

barvino.net

Basil & Wick's

Located on Route 28 in North Creek, just minutes from Gore Mountain, Basil & Wick's today bears no physical resemblance to its earlier incarnations. Rebuilt in 1999 on the site of the original Basil & Wick's, with a history dating back eight decades, about all that remains of the past are photographs, fond memories, and nostalgic tales. From 1930s dance hall to Adirondack juke joint, family, friends, and community have been a part of the Basil & Wick's story for several generations.

In homage to Basil & Wick's humble beginnings, mural-sized black-and-white photo collages hold subjects prisoners of time, depicting scenes from Gore Mountain, Whitewater Derby, and the original Basil & Wick's. Enshrined in a plexiglass case like a rare museum artifact, a chrome and vinyl barstool stands in reverence near the entrance, a relic from the early days. Backless and tattered, its emerald green seat bulges flesh-colored stuffing like an aging but sturdy sex symbol in a too-tight dress. While sentimental, it represents the future with a gracious nod to the past.

Resembling a resort ski lodge, the uncluttered timber frame with pine cathedral ceiling is cozy and inviting. A snowboard, an antique sled, skis, and an antler chandelier complete the rustic, outdoorsy theme. The bar area, known as the Lodge, houses an antique curved bar—a remnant of the famous horseshoe bar from the former Colonial Arms Hotel in Warrensburg. In contrast to so many Adirondack taverns, the Lodge at Basil & Wick's is brightly lit, with large windows and glass doors inviting natural light. Three flat-screen TVs are visible but unobtrusively placed. A flagstone fireplace provides ample warmth in winter, but regardless of the season, the atmosphere is always warm. When weather permits, dine or drink on the spacious wraparound porch. The Lodge is perfect for an intimate drink, hanging with old friends, or making new ones.

After a day of outdoor adventures, partake in Chef Chuck's

creative specialties from the full menu in the dining room, or unwind in the Lodge, where a pub menu and Happy Hour specials are featured daily from 3 to 5:30 p.m. The Drink Specials board often lists a clever martini or seasonal cocktail, and the bartenders are happy to blend something new or embellish the basics. Beer offerings, broad and well selected, include 13 draft and more than 20 bottled choices, from PBR to imports and craft beers. The wine list boasts over 30 choices by the glass or bottle.

Following changes in ownership and unsuccessful attempts by others to make a comeback under various names, Jane Peter has taken the director's seat and introduced a rising star. Not one to leave management to someone else, she is a tireless presence, but never too busy to visit with her regulars. Jane's unyielding enthusiasm and her well-chosen and creative staff are really what have put Basil & Wick's on the path to success.

Something fun always seems to be in the making, in both the bar and the restaurant. From occasional musical entertainment to the annual Donegal Beard Contest, the staff's innovative and clever ideas ensure the future success and continuity of this revived landmark. Basil & Wick's is anchored in the community of North Creek, participating in town-wide events such as the North Creek Brewfest and Gore Mountain Restaurant Week.

A homogeneous blend of local, regional, seasonal, and recreational clientele makes Basil & Wick's the perfect place to end the day, whether coming off the slopes, out of the woods, from a whitewater rafting trip, or just down the road. One visit will not be enough.

FOOTHILLS

518.251.3100

SUMMER/WINTER HOURS:

Wednesday - Monday
Open at 3 pm

OFF-SEASON HOURS:

Thursday - Monday
Open at 3 pm

CLOSED

Major holidays

HAPPY HOUR

Daily
3 to 5:30 pm

basilandwicks.com

Friends Lake Inn Wine Bar

L ocated on Friends Lake in Chestertown, just far enough from the main highways to feel secluded, this elegant country inn speaks of luxury and romance, yet carries an air of unpretentious hospitality. Screened balconies and gabled dormers emerge from the cedar shake roof of the inn's grey clapboard exterior. Like a Monet painting, the lush landscape and perennial garden invite escape to the gazebo overlooking the brook and pond. This *Wine Spectator* Grand Award-winning, AAA four-diamond-rated inn, with 17 luxury guest rooms, several dining rooms, and the Wine Bar, provides a variety of experiences.

Much more than its name implies, the Wine Bar at the Friends Lake Inn maintains that same presence, pampering guests with unparalleled service and attention to detail. Though renowned for its superior wine collection, the bar has a small but diverse beer selection and regularly serves Stella Artois, Samuel Adams seasonal, and two regional craft beers. The impressive wine menu lists at least 20 different red and white wines by the glass. A Drink Specials board includes creative mixed drink options conducive to the season. The martini menu, available upon request, offers up to 10 irresistible martinis, ranging from fruity and tropical to coffee-based. Priced at $12 to $16, one is all that's needed to put a glow in your cheeks. The Friends Lake Inn's signature L'Orange Martini sells for $22 and features Grand Marnier Cent Cinquantenaire (150th anniversary blend), Grey Goose L'Orange, fresh lemon, and organic wild clover honey. The preparations are lavish and the garnish whimsical.

Gleaming wine glasses, each polished by hand, neatly float like rows of crystal bubbles over the small but opulent bar. The bar, of beautifully crafted mission oak cabinetry with brass hardware, seats a mere eight, but the Wine Bar's dining area has tables to seat 40 to 50 guests. Two of the room's oak-paneled walls are constructed almost entirely of windows, allowing outward gaze and inward light. Stuffed leather sofas and chairs in two separate common areas invite

FOOTHILLS

518.494.4751

SUMMER/WINTER HOURS:

Monday - Friday
Open at 4 pm

Saturday - Sunday
Open at 2 pm

OFF-SEASON HOURS:

Thursday - Friday
Open at 4 pm

Saturday - Sunday
Open at 2 pm

those not afraid to relax. Though no formal Happy Hour is featured, weekly drink specials encompass mixed drinks in summer months and specialty martinis and mixed drinks in the winter season.

Much more than a bar, the Wine Bar offers appetizers of artisan cheeses, crab cakes, mussels, soups, and salads. Among entrees on the Wine Bar's seasonally evolving menu are the Friends Lake Inn signature black angus burger, the open-faced elk sandwich, and maple barbecue short ribs. On Sundays, Wine Bar dinner specials feature a selection of $7 entrées from 2 to 7 p.m.

Originally built in the 1860s, Murphy's Friends Lake Inn served as a boarding house for local tannery workers in Chestertown, later evolving into a summer getaway where city guests would escape to the lake and its secluded natural surroundings. In 1984, after sitting vacant for 15 years, the Friends Lake Inn was purchased by Greg and Sharon Taylor, who spent the next 20 years nurturing it into the premier destination that it is today. John and Trudy Phillips purchased the inn in 2004 and have continued that tradition, catering to comfort and elegance.

Inn guests, cross-country skiers, snowmobilers, and local and seasonal Friends Lake area residents are among the customary patrons. The Wine Bar at Friends Lake Inn is not for the faint of wallet, but is well worth the visit. While the inn is upscale in appearance, dress is informal. The atmosphere is charming, warm, and welcoming, and the service is superb. A perfect place for a delicious martini or a glass of fine wine, indulge your finer impulses at the Wine Bar at Friends Lake Inn.

friendslake.com

George Henry's

A *Happy Hour in the High Peaks* hometown tavern, it's difficult to review an establishment this familiar. With no first impression from which to develop a theme, a last impression will have to do.

George Henry's, on Main Street in Warrensburg, has come a long way since its heyday as the Warren Inn, where nightly brawls occurred somewhere around midnight and windows were regularly replaced. George Henry's enjoys a long history of hospitality to locals and has maintained its tradition as a stopping point for weary travelers along Route 9 to places further north. As much restaurant as bar now, it seems to invite tourists and tolerate locals.

Built on the site of the Grand Army House which burned in 1929, it was renamed the Warren Inn. Sometime in the 1980s, it changed hands and was called the Brew & Stew (or, more facetiously, the Punch & Duck), and finally George Henry's after the current owner's father and grandfather, George Henry McFarland.

Blackboards in both the dining and bar areas advertise food and drink specials as well as the upcoming musical lineup. The All-You-Can-Eat wings and Build Your Own Burger with unlimited toppings are worthy weekly specials to entice anyone out of their homes or camps on a Monday or Tuesday evening. Note that food is only served until 8 or 9 p.m., so plan accordingly. A small area of the bar is designated for the occasional band or soloist, but don't expect to do any dancing there.

The interior of the dining room, sufficiently separate to drown out bar noise and protect dining children from the barroom banter, is spacious, with tables comfortably distanced from one another. An adjacent deck provides outdoor seating during summer months. Low fencing on the busy Main Street side of the deck offers privacy and noise reduction while allowing a nice view of the Schroon River.

A newly upgraded 12-tap beer system includes domestic and regional craft beers from Lake Placid, Adirondack, Blue Point, and Southern Tier breweries. Craft bottles offer a range of choices from Apricot Wheat to IPA (by Ithaca Brewing Company), Dogfish Head, and Wolaver's. With too many to list here, check the website for the current list of craft beer options. For those whose taste runs closer to ordinary, most of the popular domestic beers are available as well. Specialty drinks aren't promoted, but George Henry's is equipped to provide the basics.

Quick Draw is available at the bar, and can also be monitored from the dining area. The pool table seems to be in use more often than not, and requires caution while en route to the restrooms during play. A jukebox and ATM complete the "recreation" area.

George Henry's has been under the ownership of the Trulli family for 25 years. With rising aspirations, owner Todd Trulli works diligently to appeal beyond the scope of George Henry's humble Warrensburg location. He is accomplishing this with a dining menu of simple yet quality offerings and a thoughtfully chosen beer menu, while popular dinner specials bring in regular clientele. Cost-conscious improvements to the partition between the bar and dining room enhance the overall experience. If any bar were to get an "A" for effort, George Henry's would be it.

When you're looking for a friendly drink or a good burger in the 'Burg, George Henry's is the place to go—a collection of locals brews, as regional as the beer and just as easily tapped. There's always something comfortable about the hometown tavern, even when it's not in your hometown.

FOOTHILLS

518.623.5186

SUMMER HOURS:

Monday - Saturday
Open at 11 am

Sunday
Open at noon

OFF-SEASON HOURS:

Monday - Saturday
Open at 11 am

Sunday
Open at noon

CLOSED

Major holidays

HAPPY HOUR

Monday - Friday
4:30 to 6:30 pm

georgehenrys.com

Indian Lake Restaurant & Tavern

C leverly disguised as a mild-mannered restaurant and liquor store, the Indian Lake Restaurant & Tavern pays homage to a classic local tavern. The beautiful antique bar of ornate columns and mirrors immediately catches the eye and looks somewhat out of place in the otherwise ordinary-looking space.

Formerly known as the Oak Barrel Tavern and Farrell's Tavern, this establishment bears evidence of several influences evolved over many decades. The bar and shelving behind it were originally part of the historic Old Nassau Tavern in Princeton, New Jersey. A restoration project in downtown Princeton called for demolition of the tavern, and a contractual agreement was drawn requiring that the bar be moved 250 miles outside the New York City area. Purchased in the 1930s, the bar was carefully dismantled and brought to Indian Lake, where it was reassembled at Farrell's Tavern and remains today. An old photograph of Farrell's Tavern reveals that little of the interior of the Indian Lake Tavern has changed since the 1940s. A framed photo of the Princeton Tiger and a dozen or so pewter mugs with Princeton names engraved still hang over the bar.

With a history dating back to the 1800s, the tavern was once an annex to a neighboring hotel, the Pelon House, long ago replaced with a parking lot. The current building housed the bar and a large dance hall that has seen its share of dancing fads come and go. It is also rumored to have been a speakeasy, disguised as an electrician's shop during Prohibition. More recently, the tavern served as "ground zero" for rafting companies and outfitters centered in Indian Lake in the 1980s, and a favorite meeting place for post-rafting adventurers to relive their experiences "rivering on the Hudson." A couple of framed photos corroborate the rafting influence.

Owners since 2005, Ann and John Miller have made various changes to accommodate the restaurant and liquor store, but still maintain the integrity of the tavern and its lengthy history. Ann and John focus primarily on making the Indian Lake Restaurant & Tavern a place to gather, reminisce, and continue the history. The restaurant and tavern close from mid-November to early December and for one month around Easter, to tidy up, perform necessary maintenance, and take a little time for vacations.

The menu features some interesting creations as well as restaurant standards. Appetizers reflect the usual bar snacks, but on closer inspection, a more extensive selection emerges, all very reasonably priced. Full dining is available in the restaurant or at the bar.

A variety of wines is available by the glass, carafe, or bottle. The adjoining liquor store offers many more wine choices, which, for a $10 corking fee, can be purchased and consumed with dinner. Draft beers are limited to Shock Top, Labatt's, Michelob Light, and Lake Placid Ubu Ale, but 24 additional bottled beers round out the assortment quite well. The Indian Lake Restaurant & Tavern's liquor arsenal allows for cocktail creativity, subject to the whim of the bartenders. The signature Apple-Ginger Martini is featured in the recipe section.

Standard amenities include a pool table tucked away toward the back and a foosball table front and center. In keeping with the times, Quick Draw and electronic golf also provide entertainment. The tavern hosts its regulars for football and NASCAR throughout the season.

The Indian Lake Restaurant & Tavern is sure to have what you're looking for while in Indian Lake. The owners, staff, and patrons create a relaxed and friendly atmosphere, earning a *Happy Hour in the High Peaks* "thumbs up."

FOOTHILLS

518.648.5115

SUMMER HOURS:

Daily
Open at 10 am

OFF-SEASON HOURS:

Daily
Open at 10 am

CLOSED

Major holidays

HAPPY HOUR

Tuesday
$1.00 off

Panther Mountain Pub

The Panther Mountain Pub, located downstairs at the Panther Mountain Inn on Route 9 in Chestertown, has been the central gathering place in Chestertown for many generations. Though now known as the Panther Mountain Pub, the bar continues to be referred to as the "P-House," as it has for so many decades.

One of the few places in the area where live music can be found on a regular basis, the Panther Mountain Pub features local and regional bands such as Willie Playmore, Cosmic Jackson, and the Steven L. Smith Band. From acoustic and blues to original and classic rock, music reverberates every Friday night throughout the year.

With an interior entrance to the pub from the 13-room inn above, as well as from a lower-level exterior parking area, the pub maintains classic features from decades ago. The bar itself, shaped like a reverse question mark, can comfortably seat 20 people, with ample room for more. The slate floor continues throughout the barroom into another back room, equipped with foosball table and shuffleboard. It's spacious enough to handle overflow from the bar, private parties, more intimate table seating, or live music and dancing. In the main bar area, a jukebox, pool table, and video games provide additional amusement. The Panther Mountain Pub is a Quick Draw retailer. Try your luck with your favorite numbers. Several TVs provide for more passive pleasures.

Originally built after the Civil War, the business was operating as a hotel named the Panther Mountain House when it burned in 1941. It was designed and rebuilt as it appears today by the Wertime family that same year. In 1957, it was purchased and run by Thomas Carroll and family until his death in 2009. The Panther Mountain Inn & Pub has been owned and operated by Keith Wilkinson and Don Butler since 2010. They have brightened up the bar area, added some trendy drink options and draft beers, and even spiced up the pub menu. The Panther Mountain Pub is affiliated with the Brant Lake Taxi service, a rare commodity in this neck of the woods, and encourages patrons to take advantage of a cab ride when necessary.

The pub is open daily at noon, serving simple pub fare, and has recently added deli sandwiches, clubs and wraps, hog wings (pork), jumbo chicken wings, and buffalo french fries with bleu cheese. The pub closes only on Christmas Day each year. Though no formal Happy Hour specials exist, the prices are very reasonable all day, every day. The bar is well stocked, but this is a beer-and-mixed-drink establishment, not recommended for fancy frozen or blender drinks. The recently added draft system, offering up to seven craft and the obligatory PBR, promises to attract more drinkers of distinction to the Panther Mountain Pub.

Centrally located on Route 9 near the intersection with Route 8, and adjacent to the Warren County snowmobile trail, the Panther Mountain Pub is likely to be occupied in the winter by sledders stopping by to warm up with a drink or a quick bite. Weekdays in winter might be quieter than weekend days, catering to locals for lunch or dinner, or those vying for an early seat for Friday's music event. During the summer, the pub is frequented by local townspeople, summer seasonal residents, inn guests, and travelers.

The Panther Mountain Pub's hometown appeal and longstanding operation attest to its tradition of serving the mainstream resident or vacationer, providing a break from the ordinary with music events and fundraisers. Patrons are typically friendly and the bar staff is attentive and professional.

FOOTHILLS

518.494.2401

SUMMER HOURS:

Daily
Open at noon

OFF-SEASON HOURS:

Daily
Open at noon

CLOSED

Christmas

panthermountaininn.com

Sporty's Iron Duke Saloon

A list of Adirondack taverns would not be complete without Sporty's Iron Duke Saloon on Route 28N in Minerva, just 40 minutes from Lake George. The scenic and winding trek along Routes 28 and 28N is the perfect ride by any means of transportation.

Utilitarian in form and structure, the log exterior presents an impression of purist practicality. The neatly kept grounds offer little in the way of ornamentation, though sense of humor and nostalgia are alluded to upon entering the huge gravel parking lot. A vintage phone booth (it works!) stands near a signpost pointing the direction and marking the distance to destinations dear to the hearts of bikers. Among them: Sturgis, Daytona, Bear Trap, and McDermott's.

Located on the former site of the Mountain View Hotel, Sporty's has been owned and operated by Dave "Sporty" Beale since 2003. Named after his longtime friend and former owner of the Wells House, William "Iron Duke" Morrisey, Sporty's Iron Duke Saloon fills a void left by the loss of Morrisey in a 1998 motorcycle accident.

Sporty's is famous for its year-round fundraisers. The calendar of events leaves no month unturned, with several featuring multiple events. They include lots of free holiday meals, auctions, helicopter rides, and annual car and bike shows. Even the ATM fees are donated to local charities.

The recent addition of The Kitchen in a new building, built separate and apart from the saloon, is yet another indication of Sporty's ingenuity, optimism, and business prowess. It can best be described as biker bar meets Friendly's. Designed to accommodate families out for a meal as much as it is to feed hungry bikers and snowmobilers, it's one of the few places within a 20-mile radius serving food and drink at noon all year long.

Obviously proud of the accomplishments and popularity of his saloon, Sporty is a gracious, gregarious, and friendly host, though one senses that he runs this place in a no-nonsense style in strict adherence to his rules. Not your everyday biker bar, Sporty's self-

FOOTHILLS

518.251.5260

SUMMER HOURS:

Daily
Noon to 2 am

OFF-SEASON HOURS:

Daily
Noon to 2 am

CASH ONLY

described "tavern, museum, and community center" supports Little League and the fire department as well, and proudly hosts the ladies of the local Red Hat Society luncheon every year. He even treats them to a ride!

Sporty's interior is as extravagant as the exterior is spartan. The "museum" is a showroom of scores of old license plates, bike parts, models, memorabilia, and photographs. Vintage motorcycles, including an *Easy Rider* replica, are cordoned off along one wall, with a tribute to Peter Fonda and the iconic film on the wall behind the bar. The tavern is large enough to accommodate the display of old bikes, a pool table, and bar and table seating.

The beverage options are straightforward. One draft microbrew is available, varying monthly, as well as a selection of bottled domestic, craft, and imported beers, "malternative" beverages, soft drinks, and tiny bottles of Sutter wines. Sporty's is also known for its bloody marys (with a pickle garnish) and white russians.

On what is quickly becoming more a campus than grounds, several neat and simple cabins are available on site for $66 per night. Camping is free ($5 for a shower). The grassy expanse features covered outdoor seating adjacent to The Kitchen, several dozen picnic tables, a pavilion, and a fire pit. With plenty to do besides drinking, outdoor activities include tetherball, horseshoes, volleyball, basketball, and hiking trails. A steep hill on the property is used for bike and snowmobile climbs during various events. Attracting bikers, skiers, hunters, and snowmobilers, Sporty's is like summer camp for adults—all year long.

sportysirondukesaloon.com

Trapper's Tavern at the Copperfield Inn

T rapper's Tavern at the Copperfield Inn is located in the business district of North Creek, within walking distance of the recently revitalized train station serving the Saratoga & North Creek Railway.

Decked out in contemporary Adirondack style, the tavern is more intimate than great room in scale. From the moose head (bagged by Teddy Roosevelt himself) peering over the stone fireplace to the timber walls and ceiling beams, there's no doubt you are in the Adirondacks. Antler chandeliers provide subtle lighting within. The tavern area consists of limited seating at the bar, with tables and upholstered rustic chairs for dining, relaxing, or listening to music when entertainment is featured. Live music is offered on Saturday in the winter and on Friday in the summer.

North Creek has so much to offer. Gore Mountain Ski Center overlooks the village, providing skiing, scenic gondola rides, mountain biking, and the Fall Festival. North Creek entertains whitewater rafters, autumn leaf peepers, and railway riders. With three bars on Main Street alone, and more nearby, North Creek is the perfect venue for a mini pub crawl. The only thing missing in North Creek is a golf course.

Clientele at Trapper's Tavern may consist of the occasional regional inhabitant, but most often is made up of skiers, outdoor enthusiasts, and probably even some golfers lost in the rough. The Copperfield Inn frequently hosts weddings, so expect the tavern to fill with wedding parties throughout the year. Guests from the Copperfield Inn's 31 rooms and suites round out the remaining population at the tavern.

The Copperfield Inn, owned by Michael Ellis, was built in 1990 on the site of the American Hotel. As is the case with so many of the Adirondacks' former hotels, it was destroyed by fire in 1903. The New American Hotel took its place in 1920. That hotel's bar, embedded with locally mined garnet, is something we would like to have seen. Trapper's Tavern was built into the Inn in 1998. The tavern was named in honor of French-Canadian trapper Jacques Dugas. The Copperfield

Inn's book, *Trapper's Tales,* recounts his adventures in tall-tale form.

After a day of outdoor adventures, settle in at Trapper's Tavern to enjoy a casual dinner and a pint or cocktail in a relaxed and rustic setting. The beer selections, while not extensive, include a variety of both bottled and draft choices in domestic, import, and craft brews. Several fine wines are also available by the glass.

The Drink Specials board and the cocktail menu at the bar consist of some delicious-sounding martinis and blender drinks. We had the good fortune to visit during the Pumpkin Martini season. The concocting of the drink created some curiosity among customers, who waited eagerly for our reactions to the first sip. More like a dessert, it was like drinking a pumpkin pie with loads of whipped cream.

The tavern menu exceeds ordinary pub-style offerings with such options as venison chili, pot pie, roasted duck breast, and the self-proclaimed "best burger in the 'Dacks." For a more formal dining experience on site, Lorenzo's specializes in Mediterranean and northern Italian cuisine prepared in the open-style kitchen. Lorenzo's is worth the look-around even if dining isn't in your plans, though it is often closed to the public for private events.

The Copperfield Inn, including Trapper's Tavern, is closed for a month in late fall, typically from mid-November through mid-December. Check the Copperfield Inn's website for the most up-to-date information. No matter the season or the reason, Trapper's Tavern is among the places to be in North Creek. Trapper's will ensnare you.

FOOTHILLS

518.251.5996

SUMMER HOURS:

Daily
Open at 11:30 am

OFF-SEASON HOURS:

Daily
Open at 11:30 am

CLOSED

Mid-November thru mid-December

HAPPY HOUR

Daily
5 to 7 pm

copperfieldinn.com

Witherbee's Carriage House

Witherbee's Carriage House on Route 9 in Schroon Lake is a bar, restaurant, and museum of local history. The parking lot holds a glimmer of what awaits discovery inside. From the display of various farm implements, wagons, and wheels surrounding the structure to the collection of wheeled conveyances inside, "carriage house" is an understatement. There's even a little red Gore Mountain gondola, skis included, hanging on the building. With so many antiques, Adirondack region memorabilia, and assorted other wonders, Witherbee's should be charging admission.

The bar is located in the loft upstairs, and even the stairs, solid chunks of aged wood, speak of times of true craftsmanship. The eye involuntarily roams among the vast collections occupying every barn-board wall, corner, crevice, and rafter. Old photographs, woodworking tools, and vintage advertising adorn the walls. Suspended from the beams above, unbelievably, are an antique carriage, a harness sulky, a hay rake, and a Victorian high-wheel bicycle, all regularly prompting questions from patrons. The loft is open, spacious, well lighted and, while packed full of "stuff," appears uncluttered and notably dust deficient. While the current collection of memorabilia is impressive, several truckloads of similar items have actually been removed. It is hard to imagine there having been even more. Witherbee's closes for its annual cleanup-closedown two weeks before Thanksgiving in order to give the place a thorough scrubbing and general sprucing up, something more establishments should consider.

The Drink Specials board boldly offers an evolving list of creative cocktails such as Pomatini, Nutcracker, and Moose Milk. The house signature, Amanda's Snickers Martini, appears in the recipe section. Moose Milk is one of Witherbee's more popular drinks. The snowmobile trail system leads right to the back door, and riders have been known to fill a thermos with Moose Milk before mounting their sleds for later enjoyment at their final destinations.

Patty and Bill Christian have owned Witherbee's since 2007. At some point around 1920, the owner at the time, George Murray, was

FOOTHILLS

518.532.9595

SUMMER HOURS:

Tuesday - Sunday
Open at 4 pm

OFF-SEASON HOURS:

Thursday - Sunday
Open at 4 pm

CLOSED

Major holidays
Two weeks in April
Two weeks in November

HAPPY HOUR

Daily
4 to 6 pm

required to move a barn that was part of the Edgewater Resort to make way for State Route 9. He is alleged to have used various influences to get the state to move it for him. The barn was converted to a restaurant named Witherbee's in the 1960s, and later operated as Terrio's for 28 years. When Patty and Bill bought it, they felt a nostalgic need to restore the original name.

A favorite among snowmobilers, summer people, and the random tourist, Witherbee's attracts a variety of clientele. Friday night bands bring in their own fan base, fundraisers draw locals, and Thursday open mic night rounds them up from as far away as Lake Placid and Ballston Spa. Witherbee's even has its own song, "Witherbee's Blues," written by local musician and open mic night host Mark Piper. In addition to regular musical entertainment, Witherbee's hosts holiday parties and the annual Murder Mystery dinner, usually to a sellout crowd.

The restaurant is well known for its Big Ass Steak and homemade soups as much as for specialty drinks, and all of the menu items are available in the loft. The smaller and more intimate main dining area is downstairs for those who prefer a quieter and more secluded experience. The bar seats 9 to 10 people, but the large upstairs has a dozen additional tables for relaxing or dining. A pool table is comfortably out of the way.

In order to satisfy the need for travelers' accommodations in Schroon Lake, Witherbee's has recently added more than a dozen rental cabins of varying capacities and amenities. Whether you're staying over or passing through, Witherbee's is a sensory smorgasbord.

Eastern Lakes Region

The Bars

Bolton
- Pub on 9

Bolton Landing
- Frederick's Restaurant & Lounge

Essex
- Essex Inn Tavern
- Old Dock House Restaurant & Marina

Lake George
- Adirondack Pub & Brewery
- Duffy's Tavern
- Judd's Tavern
- TR's Lounge at the Holiday Inn Resort

Queensbury
- Adirondack Bar and Grill

Ticonderoga
- The Burleigh House

Willsboro
- Johnny's Smokehouse & Sports Bar

EASTERN LAKES

Adirondack Bar and Grill

Barely inside the Blue Line, the Adirondack Bar and Grill, on the corner of Ridge Road and Route 149 in Queensbury, is the southernmost venue in the Eastern Lakes region of the Adirondack Park. During the summer, the bar and restaurant are most often populated with people traveling to and from eastern New York and New England. All year long, it is a favorite destination for locals and seasonal residents, who comfortably commingle with travelers at the bar.

Stuffed wildlife and mounted fish are the theme for the bar area and may well be the main topic of conversation much of the year. The polished pine slab bar top and unfinished plank walls brighten the interior and lend a piney scent. The bar offers seating for 16 to 18 patrons on comfortable vinyl stools, and several tables are dispersed around the bar, offering additional seating for overflow or just a little more privacy.

Formerly known as Len & Peg's, and as Two Squires in the 1970s, the Adirondack Bar and Grill is now owned by Jim Valastro, and has been since 2002. Outdoor events are a mainstay. Jim has recently extended the deck and has plans to add a tiki bar. The highway location and spacious, grassy backyard make it an ideal place for fundraisers and gatherings, from small, private events to huge charity benefits. The annual Wack's Ride for Wishes fundraiser draws hundreds of supporters who raise a substantial sum for the Make-A-Wish Foundation.

The expansive parking lot can readily accommodate a large crowd for any purpose, and serves as a landing and launch pad for snowmobiles in the winter. The Adirondack Bar and Grill is a popular spot on the Warren and Washington County snowmobile trails. Once the dead end of Washington County's sled route, the trail now connects with Warren County's, opening access all the way to Maine.

Single and duo acoustic entertainment is featured regularly on Fridays and occasionally on Saturdays, attracting a more varied clientele. Jim has recently dispensed with the pool table and dartboard, leaving a few TVs and Quick Draw as the only diversions beyond your drinking companions, though fellow drinkers will often engage in friendly banter on any number of subjects. If they're not particularly talkative, you can always access the free WiFi to Google *Happy Hour in the High Peaks*.

Generally a beer and basic mixed drink bar, Adirondack Bar and Grill is willing and able to accommodate some special orders, and occasionally features specialty martinis. Beer preference tends to be uncomplicated. A variety of drafts, including two craft beers, plus nearly 20 domestic and imported bottled beers and a few malt beverages, are served. For the nostalgic, Genny is a very popular choice.

Complimentary hors d'oeuvres are purported to be beyond the ordinary Happy Hour offerings. A wide selection of bar fare is served. Sandwiches, notably the roast beef *Adirondacker*, are quite popular, as are the homemade salads. The menu also includes burgers, nachos, and chicken wings, all in the $6 to $10 range. The Adirondack Bar and Grill has a separate restaurant with full dinner menu, daily lunch and dinner specials, and an outdoor dining area on the deck.

Whether stopping in for a drink, food, or both, the Adirondack Bar and Grill meets a variety of tastes and preferences. Staff and patrons are found to be pleasant company. Hunter and Adirondack outdoor writer Dan Ladd places this tavern among his favorite local meeting places any time of year, categorizing it as a "workingman's bar and a traveler's restaurant."

EASTERN LAKES

518.793.2325

SUMMER HOURS:

Daily
11 am to midnight

OFF-SEASON HOURS:

Daily
11 am to midnight

CLOSED

Major holidays

HAPPY HOUR

Monday - Friday
3 to 7 pm

adirondack-bar-and-grill.com

Adirondack Pub & Brewery

Located on Route 9 on the corner of Sewell and Canada Streets at the southern end of Lake George Village, the Adirondack Pub & Brewery's sprawling, rustic exterior and green roof are easy to spot. As much family-friendly restaurant as it is brew pub, it's truly a craft beer aficionado's destination.

The décor? You guessed it—Adirondack theme with a regional touch. Pine boughs, peeled log posts, and the requisite canoe carry on the building's exterior theme. Lake George memorabilia and photos exhibit a more personal local flavor. Over the bar, a panorama of epic proportions portrays a group of swimmers modestly clad in period swimwear. Newspaper clippings, fishing paraphernalia, animalia, and vintage regional-attraction advertising offer the eye an interesting diversion while the hand methodically, repeatedly, raises the glass. A stuffed bobcat (*not* an entrée) approves the beer menu.

If souvenirs are on your list, skip the trinket shops in the village. The Adirondack Pub & Brewery's gift area sells t-shirts, pint glasses, and the familiar "Ale so fresh, you'll want to slap it" bumper sticker. Better yet, take home a six-pack or growler of the freshest beer in town.

Owner John Carr's thirst for robust beers, and his subsequent disappointment in obtaining them, inspired him to learn the craft and create them himself. The result is a diverse selection of quality ales that have garnered awards from Glens Falls Beer Fest, Tap NY, and Battle of the Brews.

The Adirondack Pub & Brewery opened in 1999 and has expanded not only its lineup of fine brews, but its physical confines and brewing capacity as well. The brewery is one of the few that uses locally produced ingredients wherever possible, and brews, labels, and bottles its wares exclusively on site. You just can't get any more "local" than that. The beer speaks for itself through its growing demand, and the Adirondack Brewery continues to expand distribution of its products to stores, restaurants, and taverns across northeastern New York and beyond.

HAPPY HOUR IN THE HIGH PEAKS

33 Canada Street, Lake George

Serving its own beer exclusively, the Adirondack Pub & Brewery offers several varieties year-round, including Bear Naked Ale, IPA, Fat Scotsman Ale, BeaverTail Brown, Café Vero Stout, Dirty Blonde, and Bobcat Blonde. Another 14 seasonal beers keep the rotation interesting, and frequent limited-edition specialties appear for brief periods for purchase at the pub. If you're not sure where to start, try a sampler. If that's too much, the knowledgeable and friendly staff can lead you in the right direction. Not a beer drinker? Not to worry. Several wine varieties (including two from Lake George's own Adirondack Winery), basic well drinks, and specialty cocktails are options, too. The Adirondack Pub Punch is their signature drink and can be found in the recipe section.

Whether choosing from the pub menu or the dinner menu, choices are numerous, from appetizers to lunch and dinner entrees. Booth and table seating are available near the bar, and several little niches are situated farther away for a more intimate or family-centered experience. An adjoining deck, off heavily traveled Canada Street, provides outdoor seating in warmer weather.

Special events and festivals highlight all seasons at the Adirondack Brewery. The Festival of Barrels, the Bear Crawl (a six-bar pub crawl), Oktoberfest, and the Harvest Beer Dinner top the growing list of activities.

From the highly informative and attractive website to meticulously detailed product illustrations, the Adirondack Pub & Brewery demonstrates a commitment to quality and obvious pride and craftsmanship in its premium beer. At the Adirondack Pub & Brewery, beer is the public forum; you'd be remiss not to join in.

EASTERN LAKES

518.668.0002

SUMMER HOURS:

Daily
Open at noon

OFF-SEASON HOURS:

Friday - Sunday
Open at noon

CLOSED

Two weeks at Christmas

adkbrewery.com

The Burleigh House

Located at the corner of Montcalm Street and Champlain Avenue in Ticonderoga, the Burleigh House, like its predecessor of the same name, stands ready to appease the weary traveler or entertain the locals. History, industry, and recreation converge in Ticonderoga, as do the waters of Lake George and Lake Champlain.

The town is perhaps best known as the location of Fort Ticonderoga, which played a pivotal role in both the French and Indian War and the American Revolution. Pencil and paper have outlined its more recent history. The area was once a supplier of graphite for the manufacture of the famous Ticonderoga pencil, and is now home to a major paper manufacturer.

In 1953, fire destroyed the original Burleigh House. Gone was the elegant four-story hotel with its lounge and its own orchestra. A new, simpler structure replaced the original and continued as a bar and restaurant—sans orchestra. Kim Vilardo has owned the Burleigh House since 1984, when it was called "Doc's." In 2000, though no longer affiliated with the Burleigh family, the name Burleigh House was reinstated. Demonstrating her appreciation for Ticonderoga's history, Kim has collected dozens of historical photographs of the area. They are displayed in silent retrospect throughout the restaurant. Hanging over the mantel of the gas fireplace near the bar, a vintage, hand-colored, and ornately framed photograph of the original hotel paints the image best.

The Burleigh House has an allure that's difficult to define. Open and spacious, with moveable partitions for custom privacy, the interior conveys the impression of many rooms with distinct personalities. One area holds a pool table, a piano, and a few pub tables. A sitting area, with two sofas and a fireplace, provides solace in a more private setting. The bar somehow maintains a presence of the past. The contemporary style and soft, warm, cherry finish of the bar top and cabinetry suggest an opulence found in a grand hotel lounge.

The bar is separated into two sections, the smaller having long ago been claimed by regulars who deemed themselves "family." Over the years, the "family" has outgrown this space and has spread out to occupy the entire length of the bar. All patrons are now considered family.

Located equidistant from Lake Champlain and Lake George, the Burleigh House is a summer hotspot. Boaters frequently dock at Mossy Point and catch a cab to the Burleigh House, where owner or staff will often provide a complimentary ride back. The Burleigh House currently features daily Happy Hour specials from 5 to 7 p.m. and carries a diverse inventory of liquor, wine, and draft and bottled beer. Spontaneous concoctions, specialty shots, and holiday drinks regularly appear on the Specials Board.

The Burleigh House serves from its pub menu until 9 p.m. from Memorial Day through Labor Day, and outdoor patio seating is available in warmer weather. Occasional live music or a DJ, Quick Draw, off-track betting, lottery, and free WiFi are additional perks.

In either January or February of each year, the Burleigh House closes for at least a week to freshen up the décor and for owner and staff to enjoy a little time off, so check ahead if coming to visit during that time.

Local residents, outdoor enthusiasts, occasional off-season tourists, and area social clubs support the business year-round. The Burleigh House is known to host the Chamber of Commerce mixer, and the Eagles Club holds its annual fundraiser there. The local clientele are friendly and interesting and the staff will make you feel right at home. You know. Like family.

SUMMER HOURS:

Tuesday - Saturday
Open at 11 am

Sunday
Open at noon

OFF-SEASON HOURS:

Tuesday - Saturday
Open at 11 am

CLOSED

Thanksgiving
Christmas until 8 pm

CASH ONLY

HAPPY HOUR

Daily
5 to 7 pm

Duffy's Tavern

Duffy's Tavern sits in the heart of Lake George Village, not quite lakeside, between the Boardwalk Restaurant and Canada Street. Just follow the painted trail of shamrocks on the sidewalk from the corner of Canada Street to the bar. Duffy's is a great venue for entertainment indoors and out, summer and winter. With two levels and three bars, each has its own identity.

The interior is as divergent as the exterior—a mix of nautical, Irish, and beer advertising. At ground level, the primary tavern serves during all seasons. Surrounded by windows, this level allows views of the lake from the capacious bar, nearby booths, and corner niche with sofa and pellet stove. A pool table and a few electronic games provide entertainment on this floor.

Indoor and outdoor entertainment take place in the two bars located on the second floor. The large indoor area is open when bands play inside, or when the latest party dictates. An array of bar and table seating options offers views of the lake or seats near the stage. Enjoy late-afternoon acoustic music all summer long at the outdoor cabana bar. Whether you're seated at the bar or at one of many pub tables on the deck, it's one of those places where it's easy to settle in, get comfortable, and not want to leave.

Summer brings forth a variety of specialty drinks including the Lake George Iced Tea, Planter's Punch, and the Passionate Screw. The Duffle Bag appears to be a concoction of their own design—a rich and sensuous blend of vodka, peach schnapps, Southern Comfort, and orange juice. Winter fetches warmer coffee- and cocoa-based drink specials. For any season, try Duffy's signature bloody mary, featured in our recipe section. The selection of bottled and draft beers promises to please any palate.

Lunch and dinner are served daily throughout Duffy's in any area that's open. The menu lists a variety of tempting, tasty-sounding

20 Amherst Street, Lake George

appetizers and entrees, most in the $7 to $11 range. Baby back ribs, steak, chicken, homemade soups and chili, and a number of other menu items are reasonably priced. They also have a kids' menu.

Duffy's is owned and run by Mickey and Linda Duffy. Mickey's dad bought the former Sunshine Tourists rooming house in 1977 and converted it to a bar and restaurant. Mickey officially took over in 1989, but has been working the business since he was barely out of high school. A village icon, Duffy's is Lake George Winter Carnival headquarters, providing sustenance, entertainment, and warmth for participants and spectators after a day of shenanigans on the lake. Duffy's also hosts the annual Shamrock the Block party, bringing out the best of the Irish-at-heart with Celtic music, kids' activities, and a St. Patrick's Day parade.

Generally open daily throughout the year, Duffy's may change hours and days of operation as necessary, so call ahead during the off-season. As long as local laws permit, Duffy's is open daily until 4 a.m. in the summer, with live music on a regular basis. Entertainment is featured on weekends during Winter Carnival in February. Their Facebook page is a reliable source for up-to-date announcements.

Though graying around the temples, Duffy's appeals to all ages, giving Lake George area residents and visitors respite from the resort rat race for over 35 years. Music and laughter emanating from the deck often lure the passerby to Duffy's cabana bar where cool shade, a soft lake breeze, and cold drinks promise to quench the tired and thirsty. Let Duffy's reel you in too.

SUMMER HOURS:
Daily
11 am to 4 am

OFF-SEASON HOURS:
Call or visit web

CLOSED
Major holidays

HAPPY HOUR

Monday - Friday
4 to 7 pm

Essex Inn Tavern

From centuries-old brick homes and diagonal parking to waterfront buildings in colors to rival the Atlantic coast, the town of Essex has a New England charm. The Essex Inn, grand in comparative scale to the federal and Greek Revival style architecture that defines the hamlet, is the centerpiece of Essex. With a full-length front porch and imposing white columns, the Essex Inn's cheerful yellow facade smiles a sunny welcome.

Management of the Essex Inn was undertaken by Gladys and Josh Archer in 2010 following meticulous renovation and restoration by owners Rick and Karen Dalton. The inn, which has operated almost continuously for two centuries, has taken on a historic appearance that feels timeless and original. Wood is artfully employed in countless hues and textures, with rough-sawn board walls, a low exposed beam ceiling, and softly glowing wide plank floors finished with hand-forged replica nails. Wavy glass windows and a two-sided brick fireplace partition the tavern from the more formal dining area. Furnishings exhibit a distinct Adirondack flavor, contrasting smooth, polished wood with heavy, handcrafted rustic creations of twisted roots, sticks, and antlers. A thick pine slab bar, with seating for just four, overlooks rustic birch-bark cabinetry housing the bar inventory. Wait staff, all of whom are bar trained, scurry in and out of the miniscule confines, each preparing drinks for his or her own orders.

Though diminutive in size, the bar bulges with creative capacity. The Sinnfully Essex is a house specialty and is featured in the recipe section. Specialty drinks are priced at around $9. Well-selected bottled beer choices include Stella Artois, Magic Hat, Guinness, Redbridge, and Lake Placid IPA and Ubu Ale, all reasonably priced. Josh prides himself on the Essex Inn's wine selection, featuring an impressive list available by the glass or bottle, priced from the $7 a glass house wine to a $155 bottle.

Energetically revitalized and renewed with enthusiasm, Gladys and Josh have revived the essence of community in the tavern

EASTERN LAKES

518.963.4400

as a meeting place for townspeople and visitors alike. Table seating in the tavern is reminiscent of a colonial "ordinary" where one could argue politics, expound on the weather, or share gossip of local flavor. Gladys and Josh are tireless in their continuous efforts to make the Essex Inn the place to be in Essex year-round. Offering wine tastings, cooking classes, and a book-and-wine club with literary-themed dinners, new ideas are always in the works.

Themed gatherings and dinner specials, including Community Happy Hour and Martini Merdi, are among the fresh and innovative activities. On Fridays during the summer, the inn features outdoor music in the garden. In July and August, "afternoon tea" encourages a luncheon on the grass, parasols optional. Friday "prix fixe" dinners are a favorite among diners, at a price that's easy to swallow.

The Essex Inn is open for dinner Tuesday through Saturday from 5 p.m. until 9 p.m. The inn is open to guests daily, with seven rooms available. If you're just having cocktails at the bar, you should have an opportunity to meet all of the staff. Each of them seems ready and willing to try something new or share their favorite drink recipe. Gladys is a vibrant, energetic host, eager to share her obvious affection and future plans for the Essex Inn. Josh seems to remain behind the scenes, keeping the menu fresh and ensuring that all is well managed in the kitchen.

For an Adirondack experience with a hint of New England, visit the Essex Inn on the Adirondack Coast, nestled between Lake Champlain and the Adirondack Mountains. Try something new and be sure to wander around. You'll find nothing is ordinary.

SUMMER HOURS:

Monday - Saturday
5 to 9 pm

Wednesday - Saturday
Noon to 2 pm

Sunday
Noon to 7 pm

OFF-SEASON HOURS:

Tuesday - Saturday
5 to 9 pm

Friday - Saturday
Noon to 2 pm

CLOSED

Major holidays

essexinnessex.com

Frederick's Restaurant & Lounge

Bolton Landing's tiny little shop-lined Lake Shore Drive is buttoned up and battened down for much of the year. The dreary winter landscape and chilly winds off Lake George keep most tourists at bay. Springtime gradually draws proprietors from hibernation as they busy themselves with preparation for the coming season. For those who brave the winter months and remain open, business is anything but usual. It takes some creativity and loyal customers to run a four-season business in this town. Frederick's is one of those businesses.

Siblings Stuart Smith and Connie Maxam have owned and operated Frederick's Restaurant & Lounge since 1989. They have learned along the way how to survive winters in Bolton Landing and how to staff their establishment to maintain a high level of customer service all year long.

Frederick's is instantly welcoming and homey in any season. The Adirondack camp-style décor, with hardwood floors, pine board walls, and a huge stone fireplace, entices visitors to make themselves comfortable. Upholstered rustic chairs and two plump sofas invite conversation and relaxation. For socializing of a more competitive nature, a game room contains a pool table and electronic dartboard, with plenty of shelves to hold the drinks and elbows of spectators and socializers. Various mounted fish and a deer head embellish the walls. Framed photographs of Lake George capture warmer times and hold them, lest we forget.

The staff at Frederick's likes to keep boredom at bay, no matter the climate. Winter brings complimentary homemade soups and snacks during Happy Hour. Dinner specials erupt into impromptu parties. Wii bowling, karaoke nights, and the annual Super Bowl tailgate party in the parking lot highlight the winter season.

The doors to Frederick's sprawling deck open with the leaves as Bolton's businesses unzip for the bustle of the summer season. Karaoke Fridays, live Sunday music, and a raw bar all entice patrons outdoors to listen to the music and watch the boats on the lake or the people on the street. The deck has both covered and uncovered areas for basking in the sun or shelter from the rain.

HAPPY HOUR IN THE HIGH PEAKS

The bar is well stocked. Frederick's has a hearty menu of specialty drinks and a variety of domestic, imported, and craft draft beers. Frederick's even grows its own mint for mojitos. The wine list is extensive (over 50), with champagne, sparkling wine, both domestic and imported, and house wine by the glass, half-carafe, carafe, and bottle at a wide range of prices. Wine by the glass is available at affordable prices, starting at $3.75 for a house wine.

Dine at one of several tables in the lounge area or in the more private dining room. The deck accommodates up to 100 patrons for lunch, dinner, and late-night munchies. The lunch menu of soups, salads, pizza, and specialty sandwiches offers options priced at around $10. The dinner menu includes many selections from the lunch menu, as well as steaks, seafood, chicken, pasta, and even a few Mexican items. Take-out and catering are also available.

Bolton Landing is home to the world famous Sagamore Resort on Lake George and the historic Sagamore Golf Course. Fireworks displays on Lake George abound throughout the summer. Festivals, outdoor performances, and antique and craft exhibits draw people to Bolton Landing from May through September. If you stick around Bolton long enough, you may even catch a glimpse of the renowned Bolton Bed Races.

Frederick's is the ideal place to relax after a summer day at the beach or browsing the many antique shops, galleries, and boutiques. Should you find yourself in Bolton Landing in the off-season, a warm welcome awaits at Frederick's, where you're likely to meet others crazier than yourself.

EASTERN LAKES

518.644.3484

SUMMER HOURS:

Daily
Open at noon

OFF-SEASON HOURS:

Monday - Friday
Open at 4 pm

Saturday - Sunday
Open at noon

CLOSED

Major holidays

HAPPY HOUR

Monday - Friday
4 to 6 pm

fredericksrestaurant.com

Johnny's Smokehouse & Sports Bar

S till in its infancy, Johnny's Smokehouse & Sports Bar on Route 22 in Willsboro seems poised for longevity. The combination of exciting and creative menu options, a wide selection of beverages, and an appealing atmosphere contribute to an overall enjoyable experience you'll want to repeat. Established by Trisha Sheehan in 2011, Johnny's was named after her father. Whether he loaned her some money or she's making retribution for childhood antics, we will never know.

Willsboro, founded in 1765, is named after its founder, William Gilliland. Fortunately, some thought appears to have gone into which moniker would be best suited for the town's name. A town whose economy long revolved around limestone and paper industries, Willsboro and its nearby communities of Essex and Westport now rely primarily on tourism centered on Lake Champlain. Traveling Route 22 between Westport and Keeseville, Johnny's is a welcome change from the typical roadside bar.

Located just outside of Willsboro, Johnny's is a roadhouse by definition and location. But banish images of a tumbledown, road-weary wayside dive. Evidence of former occupancy by a Mexican restaurant is masked but not missing in the building design. Freshly painted stucco, appealing arched windows, and an entry trimmed in taupe accent Johnny's unique façade. On the inside, the appearance is light, airy, and fresh. Pub tables boldly display Johnny's logo emblazoned on each. Walls are decorated in warm, cheerful hues of persimmon trimmed in a soft grey. The bar, in alternating stripes of cherry and maple and accented with embedded casino chips, accommodates 8–10 on padded wooden stools.

A wide-screen TV occupies each corner of the pub area, presenting views from all areas of the room. For the multi-tasker, or those rare occasions when nothing is on, electronic darts, a jukebox, and Quick Draw serve to amuse. A back wall of recovered barn board is a contrasting rustic accent and serves as a partition between bar and restaurant. Barn doors on wrought iron hinges swing open to unite the bar with the dining area for Johnny's occasional DJ or live music. An enclosed patio holds six tables topped with umbrellas for outdoor dining or cooling off on a summer evening.

Johnny's is on the snowmobile trail and there's no better place for winter comfort than a smokehouse. Johnny's keeps its two smokers busy making their own cured meats on site. Oh the food you can eat! It's a smokehouse of meat! The Smokehouse Sampler is a great way to introduce yourself to Johnny's. Slather with homemade sauces and enjoy. The range of food choices is vast: salads with homemade dressings, wings, burgers, sandwiches, mac & cheese bites, homemade desserts, and even several vegetarian selections. Johnny's also hosts on-site events and offers take-out, delivery, and catering.

Happy Hour specials include discounted draft beers and well drinks, and half off a second appetizer. Beer flows freely at Johnny's, but don't hesitate to ask for your favorite mixed or frozen drink. The bartenders are capable mixologists too, frequently shaking creative martinis and cosmos. Johnny's Mountain Melon Ball appears in our recipe section. Assorted wines, malt beverages, five draft beers, and 30 bottled beers and coolers complete the beverage menu.

Visit Johnny's website for information on upcoming specials, events, and celebrations. During holidays, expect both staff and bar to be equally dressed in festive attire.

Johnny's has its share of diverse patrons, including locals, tourists and seasonal residents. Not just a restaurant. Not just a sports bar. A place to go alone, bring along your friends, make new friends, have a drink, and try something new. Meet, greet, eat, and repeat.

EASTERN LAKES

518.963.7427

SUMMER HOURS:

Monday - Thursday
Open at 4 pm

Friday - Sunday
Open at 11:30 am

OFF-SEASON HOURS:

Sunday
Open at 1 pm

Monday; Wednesday thru Saturday
Open at 4 pm

CLOSED

Christmas

HAPPY HOUR

Monday - Friday
4 to 6 pm

johnnyssmokehouse.com

Judd's Tavern

Judd's Tavern, located on Canada Street in the center of Lake George Village, beckons to the casual passerby as an ideal place to take a break from browsing the surrounding gift shops and arcades, duck in for a cool respite from the beach, or catch up on the day's sporting events.

Some sports bars are so huge that patrons could spend hours and not speak to anyone outside their social sphere. Judd's isn't large, but is of sufficient size to make it a comfortable place to meet others. Brick red walls and natural wood subdue the light spilling through the street-side row of windows. The red and white checkerboard tile floor surrounding the 16-seat bar adds a bit of fun and brightens the room. Carpeting and a suspended ceiling help keep this narrow space from being too noisy. Seating is limited to the bar and a handful of pub tables near the windows and between the game tables. A ledge running the full length of one wall provides additional space for resting beverages.

Owned by Judd Gershen, Judd's Tavern has been in business since 2004. A standard sports bar for locals and tourists, 12 TVs broadcast just about every contest that's being televised at the moment. They're not big screen, but Judd's isn't that big. Games and activities include foosball, a pool table, and a jukebox. Musical entertainment is featured sporadically.

But really, this place is all about the beer. A revolving selection of craft draft and bottled beers from the likes of Alesmith, Duval, Southern Tier, and Ithaca brewing companies makes an impressive lineup. Find a favorite among the drafts and fill a growler to go. Judd's routinely keeps four to five Dogfish Head varieties on tap and several more in bottles, but the semi-annual Dogfish Head Tap Takeovers are not to be missed! The mass-distributed "big beer" companies enjoy representation as well with at least a dozen domestics consistently stocked in bottles.

The constantly changing specialty drink list puts Judd's a notch above your standard sports bar. From the Birthday Cake Martini to the Sandy Bay Slammer, bartenders obviously enjoy getting back to their mixologist roots. Both the Veggie Mary and the Spicy Mary are sure to satisfy the bloody mary connoisseur. Judd's keeps the creativity flowing, not just the beer.

When it comes to food, the menu is limited but well done. Judd's is not a full-service restaurant, but serves assorted munchies, sliders, and is notorious for wings (which, of course, are the "best in town"). The 13 varieties include Caribbean Jerk, Aloha, Mesquite, and Wings of Fury (for which you will have to sign a waiver). The quesadillas, nachos, and fried pickles are equally enticing.

They might scale back the hours in winter by opening a little later, but Judd's is there when you need it most. The best time to visit is anytime during the summer and on Sundays during football season, when you will find every NFL game that's televised. The tavern is closed for a week in late September or early October and again for a week in March. Judd's is usually open on holidays, but be sure to check ahead if planning to visit on a major holiday. Call or visit their Facebook page for events and closings.

With accommodations available all over Lake George, Judd's caters to foot traffic in summer, and in winter during the annual Winter Carnival. The clientele tend to be mostly local, but visitors are encouraged and welcome by the affable and knowledgeable staff. No need to wait for a big event. Make your own at Judd's Tavern.

EASTERN LAKES

518.668.2554

SUMMER HOURS:

Daily
Open at noon

OFF-SEASON HOURS:

Monday - Thursday
Open at 4 pm

Friday - Sunday
Open at 1 pm

CLOSED

One week in March
Last week in September

HAPPY HOUR

Monday - Friday
4 to 7 pm

Old Dock House Restaurant & Marina

Slip into your sandals, favorite Hawaiian shirt, or bold summer skirt, and escape to an Adirondack oasis at the Old Dock House Restaurant & Marina in Essex. You may find yourself humming the theme from *Gilligan's Island* as you approach the cheerful, barn-red building with a small boat shipwrecked into the structure.

The main bar area, housed in an add-on shed, is so enclosed it's hard to tell you're outside but for the light breeze that travels through. The explosion of nautical-themed debris strewn throughout the barroom invokes a Florida Keys flashback, with a craving for rum or coconut or anything tropical.

This is a bar we have to categorize as one of our museum finds. The décor appears to be a salvage operation in progress. Odd posts and lintels serve aesthetic, if not structural, purpose. Randomly scattered fishing buoys and markers bob from walls and ceiling in a conglomeration of color. Moored on shelves, model sailing vessels pick up breezes in their sails, using their most effective lines. The bar of distressed hardwood, seemingly recovered from a bowling alley on a sunken ship, is illuminated by white enamel barn lights dangling overhead. Another side bar runs the entire length of the room and could easily seat 20, with an unhindered view through wide screened openings. An abandoned bird's nest is inconspicuously tucked into the safety of the eaves. Nearby, a red rooster observes quietly, too lazy to crow for day.

Each dining area is unique in form, seating, and table design. The open and spacious interior dining room with soaring beam ceiling contains the other half of the exterior bar, with stool seating for eight. Large, top-hinged awning windows afford a view of the ferry landing. Panoramas of Lake Champlain and the Adirondack and Green Mountains are visible through a wall of glass doors, or on the wraparound patio. In a profusion of red, tables of an assortment of

SUMMER HOURS:

Daily
Open at 11 am

CLOSED

November thru April

materials—wrought-iron mesh, one of granite, and some of wood—are scattered inside and out, with chairs of wood, plastic, and more wrought iron. Large canopies cover many of the tables, providing protection from the elements. Between patio and bar, under the shade of maples and away from the sun's burning gaze, several booths accommodate seating for 10, benches stretching at least 8 feet in length.

Originally built as a wharf in 1810 for Lake Champlain boat traffic delivering goods from Albany and New York City, the Old Dock House served as a tearoom in the 1930s. The restaurant has been in business for 30 years, run by Black Bart Bailey from the 1960s to 1983. It was restored in the mid-1980s by Joanne and Jack Halpin, who added the boat slips. It's still owned by Jack Halpin, but has been operated by Steve McKenna since 2007.

HAPPY HOUR

Daily
4 to 6 pm

The bar, restaurant, and marina are open daily from May through October, serving lunch at 11:30 a.m. and dinner from 5 to 9 p.m. The restaurant offers full dining, and a bar menu features appetizers, salads, steamed clams and lobster, and shellfish pie.

Happy Hour is daily, from 4 to 6 p.m., with draft beer and mixed drink specials. The bartenders are willing and able to mix up just about any drink you might want. We found inspiration here for the Essex Escape, which is included in our recipe section.

Located right next to the Charlotte-Essex Ferry landing, the Old Dock House is a perfect escape, whether arriving by car, boat, or ferry. If for no other reason, go for the view. Drink in the surroundings as you drink in the surroundings.

olddockrestaurant.com

Pub on 9

Open since January 2012, the Pub on 9 is the youngest pub in our 46er lineup. Located south of the village of Bolton Landing, the Pub on 9 is on Route 9N, or Lake Shore Drive, between Diamond Point and Bolton Landing. Set back a comfortable distance from the road, with a well-suited parking area and a large deck in front, the pub is a perfect spot for entertainment, indoors or out.

If we had to use one word to describe the Pub on 9, the word would be "big." From the oversized bar, enormous rooms, and 70-inch television, to the 9 Dog and the 9 Burger, everything is big at the Pub on 9. The Pub on 9's three-sided bar is stocked with all of the necessities: an abundant draft beer selection (10 flavors), coolers full of bottled beers, and much more than the basics on the liquor shelves.

The open floor plan flows seamlessly from bar, to dining, to a large game room, creating separate but inclusive spaces throughout. Three TVs suspended stadium style above the bar allow viewing from all sides, and there's another in the game room. The monster flat screen may be best viewed from a comfortable club chair in the dining area, but can be seen from pretty much everywhere.

The 9 Burger, a food consumption challenge, is made of one full pound of meat, including a quarter pound of ham topped with bacon, onions, and cheese. Finish the entire colossal burger and plate full of fries (coleslaw and pickle optional) to claim a free t-shirt and bragging rights. If super-sized food specialties aren't for you, hand-cut fries and homemade soups are very popular. Plenty of normal-sized options are found on the menu and range from $7.99 to $12.99, to eat in or take out. Their signature drink, the 9-Tini, is described in our recipe section, but is not a take-out option.

The atmosphere is simple, clean, and spacious. Pine predominates, from walls to ceiling. Decoration mostly consists of mirrored beer advertisements and a neon Welcome to Bolton sign. The smell of popcorn permeates the room. Despite its size, the Pub on 9 somehow manages to feel cozy.

Not much is happening in Bolton Landing in the winter, but the Pub on 9 keeps busy entertaining the locals and the curious. The generous dance floor rocks with musical entertainment on Saturday nights, and on occasional Fridays, too. Wing Night (with "celebrity" bartender) and Mexican Night are just a few of the specials offered at Pub on 9 throughout the year.

For the latest offerings, a calendar of events is posted regularly on their website. When planning to visit, keep in mind that the Pub on 9 closes for the month of March, but is open for all holidays that fall on their scheduled open days, with the exception of Christmas Day.

Formerly known as the Wooden Barrel, the Pub on 9 is now owned by Bob and Noelle Schwab. The Schwabs have applied personal touches to make this pub their own, stopping short of removing the barrels that protrude from the exterior wall.

Owners and staff are friendly and attentive. They take pride in the establishment and are eager to inform or amuse. The Pub on 9 doesn't open until 5 p.m., so they cater to the after-work crowd off-season and the after-a-big-day-of-touristy-stuff visitors in the summer. Both tired and hungry, all are greeted by fresh and lively staff. Dinnertime or anytime, always a great time at Pub on 9.

EASTERN LAKES

518.644.7023

SUMMER HOURS:

Wednesday - Sunday
Open at 5 pm

OFF-SEASON HOURS:

Thursday - Saturday
Open at 5 pm

CLOSED

Month of March
Christmas

HAPPY HOUR

Daily
5 to 7 pm

pubon9.com

TR's Lounge at the Holiday Inn Resort

L ocated just south of the village in the town of Lake George, TR's (Teddy Roosevelt's) Lounge at the Holiday Inn Resort is one of the highest peaks in Lake George and affords a bird's-eye view from its perch on a hill overlooking the lake. Home to local regulars who gather to catch up with family news and prognosticate about town politics, there exists a camaraderie among fellow residents who freely flow throughout the room or talk across the bar. Bartenders greet the vast majority of customers by name. Newcomers and hotel guests are made to feel equally at home and are frequently introduced to the regular patrons, with whom they always seem to find something in common.

There has been a bar at the Holiday Inn since it was built in 1966. The inn has changed hands only once since then, in 1990, and is now owned by Mike Hoffman and ably run by General Manager Michael Spilman. In 2009, the hotel and bar were extensively renovated and remodeled, earning resort status. Consistently ranked among the top Holiday Inns in the country, much-deserved honors and awards have been bestowed on this resort. The Holiday Inn is home to the Lake George Dinner Theater, entertaining audiences for over four decades. Production takes place from mid-July to late October, and TR's is the pre-performance stage for a pick-me-up.

It's tough to shake the "hotel lobby" effect of most hotel bars, but TR's manages to almost pull it off with accents of its own individuality. The bar is contemporary and sophisticated in design, neither too stark nor too trendy, with warm-toned woodwork and window moldings. Framed landscape photographs grace the linen-textured walls, while oversized drum pendant lamps float overhead. Overlooking Lake George, a wall of windows brightens the room as sunlight coaxes warm reddish hues from the woodwork and lustrous granite bar. The bar seats 18 in cider-stained slat-back bar stools with woven leather seats, the U shape conducive to conversation. Window-side pub tables and several small dining tables provide additional seating. During the milder season, enjoy remarkable views around the firepit on the outdoor patio.

The bar is completely separate from the restaurant, but a pub menu and Happy Hour appetizers are served daily. Following a longstanding Happy Hour tradition, complimentary hot hors d'oeuvres are provided, with a different item featured every day of the week. Drink prices are reasonable, the liquor selection is adequate, and the beer and wine choices are sufficient, though bartenders at TR's frequently shake up a menu of specialty cocktails. The TR's Lounge signature cocktail, Bully for Watermelons!, is detailed in the recipe section. Wines include red, white, sparkling, and champagne. Coors and Samuel Adams seasonal drafts and 16 bottled beers vary in price by brand and size. Draft beers are served in either a 16-ounce or a whopping 23-ounce glass.

The regulars are pretty serious about their football and NASCAR, and TR's has free weekly football or NASCAR pools. If the locals aren't entertainment enough, two oversized TVs and Quick Draw provide diversion. Just ask for the daily code if you need WiFi, whether you're a guest at the hotel or just stopping by the bar.

With an upscale look and a hometown heart, TR's Lounge is a mingling of locals and hotel guests; the trick is telling which is which. The bartenders are genial, personable, and professional. The patrons are equally friendly and won't hesitate to start or join a conversation. Happy Hour at TR's is full of smiles—from both sides of the bar.

EASTERN LAKES

518.668.5781

SUMMER HOURS:
Daily
Open at noon

OFF-SEASON HOURS:
Daily
Open at noon

HAPPY HOUR
Daily
4 to 7 pm

lakegeorgeturf.com

Southern & Sacandaga Region

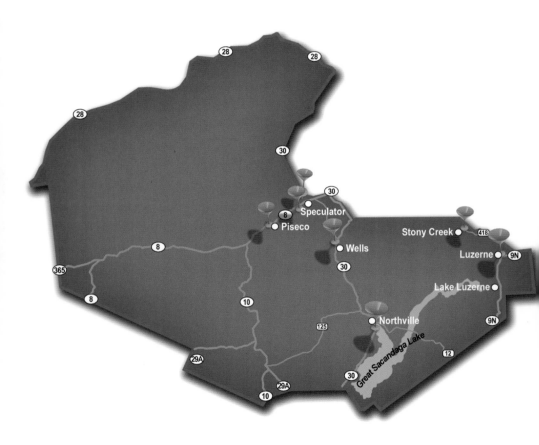

The Bars

Lake Luzerne
- Long Horn Restaurant & Pub

Northville
- Sport Island Pub

Piseco
- Oxbow Inn

Speculator
- Inn at Speculator
- Melody Lodge Tap Room

Stony Creek
- Stony Creek Inn

Wells
- Lake House Grille

SOUTHERN & SACANDAGA

Inn at Speculator

The Inn at Speculator has been the McGovern family business since Neil and his wife Linda moved to Speculator in 1979. Neil tells an amusing story about Linda's reaction that first year in the Adirondacks, when record snowfalls made her want to rethink their North Country future. Linda now handles operations behind the scenes, and their son, Eric, is the chef and manager. Neil's role seems to be chief historian and storyteller.

In keeping with a building from the mid-1900s, a series of rooms adjoining the bar area add more dining space away from the bar. A glass case in the front room displays the inn's homemade gourmet dressings and books for sale on the history of the inn. It appears to have once been a place to pay your tab on the way out, to get change for games or the jukebox, and may have offered candy or souvenirs for sale. The décor is distinctly rec room, with hardwood floors and bootleg pine-paneled walls covered with photos, certificates, and memorabilia. Linda's attempts at Victorian embellishment seem fraught with resistance. She perseveres.

The *Rogue's Gallery* is a photographic testimony to local events and characters—most notably, Jimmy the house detective. A commanding presence (and pretty snappy dresser) with a reserved demeanor, Jimmy was a long-term guest and often mistaken as the owner. Exhibiting an atmosphere of family entertainment from the past, the Inn at Speculator now entertains the adults with a pool table, foosball, electronic darts, Quick Draw, and an occasional solo musician or DJ. For the sports fan, there are three TVs in the bar area. Football, NASCAR, and March Madness basketball pools help the staff and patrons through the long winter months, though it's likely little consolation for Linda.

Liquor basics, a handful of draft beers, and 18–20 mostly domestic bottles provide adequate thirst-quenching options. Seasonal drinks of the coffee variety in winter and refreshing coolers in the summer are subject to the creativity of the bartender. The Inn at

SOUTHERN & SACANDAGA

518.548.3811

SUMMER HOURS:

Tuesday - Sunday
Open at 11 am

OFF-SEASON HOURS:

Thursday
Open at 4 pm

Friday - Tuesday
Open at 11 am

CLOSED

Major holidays
One week in April

HAPPY HOUR

Monday - Friday
4 to 6 pm

Speculator's Adirondack Citrus Cooler is described in the recipe section.

The pub room serves lunch and pub fare until the main dining area opens at 5 p.m. The kitchen usually closes at 9 p.m., but occasional late-night specials keep it open later. Neil describes some of their most popular dinner items—angus steaks, veal specialties, and seafood—as "stuff your wife won't cook."

Speculator is a summer and winter destination. Nearby, Lake Pleasant attracts summer tourists and Oak Mountain entertains skiers. Neil and Linda sponsor community events and fundraisers throughout the year, including an ice-fishing tournament in February, fish and game club events, and local snowmobile club activities. Four rooms are available for lodging, with special rate packages varying throughout the year. Rooms possess neither TV nor phone, but a television is located in a common room and cell phone service is accessible throughout the inn.

If you're looking for a quaint, overpriced Adirondack country inn filled with antiques, bark furniture, and faded sepia photographs, keep looking. Instead, you will discover a roadside rest more representative of today's residents—true Adirondackers who struggle to make a living in an area that relies heavily on tourism. Here, icons of a playground for the affluent are replaced with images of friends and neighbors doing the things they enjoy—fishing, hunting, snowmobiling, skiing, and celebrating their customary events—in a town they love and care about. Sit at the bar with the locals as they debate park politics and banter about the everyday. You'll be accepted. And listen. Learn something. If only what it's like to live here.

Lake House Grille

O wned since 2006 by Frank Mesiti, whose dad bought the building when it was a convenience store, the Lake House Grille in Wells has established itself as a notable restaurant and music venue. The population in Wells triples in the summer, with an influx of summer-home part-timers, tourists, and retirees flocking to Wells and Lake Algonquin.

A patio in front of the Lake House Grille is partitioned from the sidewalk by a fence of varying height, with windows built into the taller portions. Within the enclosure, several metal tables with umbrellas and a few Adirondack chairs provide seating for dining, relaxing, or listening to the music from within.

The bar, an island situated in the center of the room, is surrounded by 12 Windsor stools painted violet blue. Hand-thrown earthenware mugs dangle patiently over the bar, awaiting liberty at their Mug Club sponsors' whims. Purposely not rustic in theme, art, music posters, and photographs impart a flavor of funkiness as an eclectic fusion of music plays quietly in the background. Walls of soft, rag-painted sand and ivory with arts-and-crafts amber wall lanterns suggest a sense of subtle style. Barely visible, but noticeably out of place, hangs a tiny (six inches tiny) plastic deer head, inscribed, "The Lake House not Adirondacky enough for you? Then here's our Adirondack flair."

A generous dose of humor is served with tongue planted firmly in cheek. A glance at the menu informs that separate checks are not provided, but a calculator will be. Further reading reveals the Punch You in the Rye burger, the Tree Hugger, and Holy Cow! Bon Jovi 'Chovi and Smokin' Floyd pizzas enlist the backup of musical guests. Starters, salads, and sandwiches all promise a fresh and tasty deviation from the norm and are all priced between $5 and $15.

Beer and wine are the only potent choices at the Lake House

SOUTHERN & SACANDAGA

518.924.2424

SUMMER HOURS:

Daily
5 to 10 pm

CLOSED

Columbus Day to
Memorial Day

CASH ONLY

Grille. The wine list starts with the Black Box line of—you guessed it—boxed wines, dispensed through a wine cask mounted on the wall. Now wait. Before wrinkling your nose in snobbish distaste, and in its defense, Black Box wines have garnered gold medals in nationwide competitions and, since air can't get in, it stays fresher longer. Three California wines are listed at $17 to $20 for a full bottle, and six are available in half bottles for $12 to $16. A hand-printed chalkboard menu lists various microbrews served by the pint. The choices vary, representing regional microbreweries such as Ithaca Beer Company, Lake Placid Brewery, Long Trail, and Shipyard. Unless you'd prefer the Miller Lite.

The Lake House Grille has added a new stage to better accommodate the lineup of talented musicians. From blues to southern rock, bluegrass to jazz, and back again, entertainment is featured every Saturday night at 8 p.m. and, in August, is expanded to include Fridays. Some notables returning every year are Sean Rowe, George Fletcher, Tequila Mockingbird, and Tony Markellis. (You can decide who's notable.) Live traditional Irish music plays on Thursdays in the summer.

The Lake House Grille's season is short, but it's a full jam session. Open from Memorial Day to Columbus Day weekend, you'll want to work this one into your schedule.

Frank's enthusiasm for music and food diverge from the typical offerings of the local bar scene. He has created a unique and simple, yet inspired, little niche in Wells. His personable, easy personality, and attention and interest in his business and customers, have helped Frank to nurture dedicated fans. He can count on many more.

lakehousegrille.com

Long Horn Restaurant & Pub

The Long Horn Restaurant and Pub at Lake Vanare in Lake Luzerne has been owned by Jeremy and Shannon Carner since 2009. A portion of the building dates back to 1947, when the tavern was known as the Totem In. Various enterprises have come and gone since then, and much has been added to the structure. The Long Horn has matured into a charming tavern and restaurant with exceptional features, both physical and psychological, by following a few simple rules.

Enlist a solid support system. Situated right off the area snowmobile trail, the Long Horn presumes a snowy season each winter. Summer months attract vacationers and motorcyclists to nearby Lake Vanare and Fourth Lake, but even visitors from more distant Lake George find their way to the Long Horn. Tourists are lured by campgrounds and an assortment of motels, cabins, and vacation homes in the Lake Vanare area. A few dude ranches draw even more attention. Several river rafting and tubing ventures are located in the area, promising adventure on the waters of the Hudson and Sacandaga Rivers.

Appearances are important. The Long Horn exterior bears a rustic wood and brick countenance. Patios enclose the front of the building for use as weather permits, and picnic tables remain all year long. Arriving through the bar entrance, the eye is drawn to a specials board mounted on the back side of a large fireplace. The fireplace is the heart of both rooms, complemented by slate and hardwood floors. Log rafters and pine-paneled walls convey a country cordiality. Painted footprints decorate the ceiling over the bar, identifying walking patterns of the lynx, coyote, deer, and skunk in terms of ordinary gait, easy lope, and walk. Pub tables fill both sides of the room, moderately distanced from the bar. The dining room, with its own fireplace, is separated from the bar to afford a quieter atmosphere. A pool room adjacent to the bar offers enough seclusion to play a serious game and still be a part of the scene. XM Radio plays at just the right

HAPPY HOUR IN THE HIGH PEAKS

SOUTHERN & SACANDAGA

518.696.5655

SUMMER HOURS:

Wednesday - Monday
Open at 4 pm

OFF-SEASON HOURS:

Wednesday - Thursday
Open at 4 pm

Friday - Sunday
Open at 11 am

CLOSED

Major holidays
One week in April

volume in the background.

Everyone has something to contribute. A diverse liquor stock and over 40 choices of bottled and draft beer make an impressive showing. Specialty drinks like the Almond Kiss and Peppermint Pattie show initiative. The Long Horn also has a Mug Club with members' only discount benefits. Drink specials appear spontaneously.

Never underestimate the power of creativity. The Long Horn's menu is as varied as it is creative. Evidence of the influence of Deadheads is discreet, but menu items cleverly named after Grateful Dead songs, a small framed drawing of Jerry Garcia, and a skull hidden above the fireplace quietly suggest you are among friends. The lunch menu of sandwiches and burgers is available all day, and dinner is served from 5 p.m. until the kitchen closes at 9 p.m.

Involvement builds character. There is always something happening at the Long Horn. A pool league meets on Thursday during the winter. All year long, Wednesday is Trivia Night and Thursday is reserved for Beer Bar Bingo. On Friday, a littleneck-clams special entertains the palate. Live bands play on Friday and Saturday nights. Check the Long Horn's website for the latest specials and music schedule.

Everyone deserves a little pampering. The Long Horn does close for a week in April. The Carners use that time to give the place a good cleaning, make necessary repairs, and generally freshen up for a new season. If there's any time left, they take a vacation.

Regardless of what initially lures you to the Long Horn, the attraction will last a lifetime.

**thelonghornrestaurant
andpub.com**

Melody Lodge Tap Room

rrival at the Melody Lodge in Speculator presents an immediate quandary. It's difficult to decide what to look at first—the incredible hilltop views or the rustic grandeur of an authentic Adirondack lodge. From the upper parking lot, a panoramic view of Lake Pleasant and Sacandaga Lake stretches across the horizon. The barn-red Melody Lodge, a rustic, two-story structure wrapped in a porch of stone columns, stands as the centerpiece in this picturesque frame. The columns of seemingly haphazard piles of stone authenticate the craftsmanship of earlier days. Several outdoor tables and white Adirondack chairs on the porch and lawn offer lengthy scenic views.

Melody Lodge was originally built in 1912 as a singing school for girls, and operated until World War I, when the school closed and it became a private residence. In 1937, Melody Lodge was opened to the public for meals and lodging. In 1976, it was acquired by Susan and George Swift. The Swifts ran the lodge until 2006, when Julie Atty and her husband, Kyle, took over its operation.

The lobby is a cozy common room with a sofa and chairs drawn to a fireplace. Paneled glass walls partition the dining room that expectantly awaits the dinner bell. Another stone fireplace, of massive proportions, is the focal point of the dining room. Telltale noises and voices beckon from another direction, indicating the possibility of a pub.

The tavern's multi-level floor plan draws attention upon entrance to what Melody Lodge calls the Tap Room. The bar seats 10, with pub and dining tables in nearby formation. Rows of white earthenware mugs assemble in rank overhead, covering nearly the entire ceiling over the bar. With over 250 members in Melody Lodge's Mug Club, no new members are being recruited at this time. A curious square game board called ring toss hangs on the wall, scuffed and worn with obvious decades of enjoyment.

A 10-point buck's head peers from the lower level, keeping

HAPPY HOUR IN THE HIGH PEAKS

SOUTHERN & SACANDAGA

a watchful eye on the bar. A regulation shuffleboard table consumes one whole wall on this level. Several dining tables and two stuffed chairs in a comfy sitting area provide seating away from the bar.

The Tap Room has its own pub menu of appetizers, salads, soups, and entrees available all day. Rack of lamb, Steak by George, roast duck, seafood, and pasta highlight the dinner menu and may be ordered at the bar once the dining room opens at 5 p.m. Appetizers include lamb lolly-chops, clams in ale, and buffalo shrimp. Finish with a homemade dessert before the kitchen closes at 9 p.m.

Melody Lodge's location near Sacandaga Lake and Lake Pleasant provides breathtaking vistas in an old-world setting, no matter what the season. Summer brings tourists to Speculator for hiking, fishing, and boating. In winter, snowmobilers gather in boisterous groups, eager to grab lunch and a drink before moving on to the next stop. The annual Snow Dance, held on the first Saturday in December, celebrates the coming of winter with a bonfire and live music. The Lodge offers seven guest rooms, each uniquely named for a musical instrument, promising private baths for today's standards.

The Melody Lodge is more a visitor's haven than a hangout for locals, but the exchange of greetings between the bartender and the coming and going customers make it clear that many patrons stop in regularly. There are some venues that warrant a visit for no other reason than to see them for yourself. Melody Lodge is just such a place—inviting and warm, without pretense, and well worth visiting.

518.548.6562

SUMMER HOURS:

Sunday
Open at noon

Monday
Open at 4 pm

Wednesday - Saturday
Open at 11:30 am

OFF-SEASON HOURS:

Sunday
Open at noon

Wednesday - Saturday
Open at 11:30 am

CLOSED

Month of April
Month of November

melodylodge.com

Oxbow Inn

Like so many of the roadhouses tucked away in the Adirondacks, the Oxbow Inn, on Route 8 in Piseco, is genuine and unapologetic. Pieced together with no particular theme in mind, the interior spans decades of decorative tastes. The veneer-topped bar is built on a glass-block base, the floor is linoleum tile, and the walls are pine. Hinged interior storm windows serve more decorative than energy-efficient purpose. A variety of memorabilia, humorous signs, and the season's line of Oxbow fashions fill the walls and area behind the bar. A hand-painted saw blade depicts the old country inn in its serene lakeside setting.

The Oxbow Inn's location on Oxbow Lake allows lakeside entrance by snowmobile or watercraft. Oxbow Lake is a mile-long freshwater lake that offers tranquility seldom found on a roadside lake. With an average depth of 10 feet, it is favored for ice fishing, but attracts other predators like Ospreys, Great Blue Heron, loons, and a variety of ducks. The omnipresent Oxbow Mountain and the Jessup River Wild Forest Area ensure pristine views for years to come.

Owned by Heather Sboto, the Oxbow Inn is one of Piseco's (and Hamilton County's) oldest, continuously operating establishments, surpassing 100 years. Heather, as her youth will attest, has only been operating the bar and restaurant since 2008, but is comfortable and adept at filling the shoes of Oxbow keepers past and facilitating the exchange of information among bar patrons—be it snowmobile trail conditions or where the fish are biting.

The Oxbow is ready for any number of guests. The 14-seat bar spans most of the length of the tavern area, and an additional pub table provides a view of the parking lot and busy Route 8. The bar can become crowded and noisy, especially during special events. Burgers are notoriously popular among the numerous lunch, dinner, and appetizer choices. Summertime brings out occasional Mexican Night specials with Coronas, margaritas, and tasty Mexican dishes.

Route 8, Piseco

Lake-view seating, in either the dining room or on the deck, provides a quieter option away from bar banter and raucousness.

Most drinking here is without fanfare, but the Shot-of-the-Day can be found on the Drink Specials board on Saturdays, along with several other creative suggestions. Our offer to invent a signature drink was readily accepted and quickly renamed from slammer to martini, kicking the class meter up a notch. The Oxbow Martini, comprised of orange vodka, cranberry juice, and a splash of 7-Up, proved to be a tasty beverage worthy of the Oxbow name. If that doesn't appeal to you, a well-rounded liquor selection and plenty of bottled and draft beers will quench your thirst.

Aside from your bar mates, diversions are limited. Electronic darts is the only game in town. The jukebox is willing and able to transition from rock to country music at the drop of a coin. Cell service is sporadic, with Verizon reputedly outperforming AT&T.

With direct access to snowmobile trails, the Oxbow is winter headquarters for the Pleasant Riders Snowmobile Club. Groomers frequently gather to report on trail conditions. Snowmobilers come seeking food or drink, but mostly to talk about the trails. The club's annual winter Tree Burning Party includes an outdoor barbecue, bonfire, fireworks, and live music.

A trendy stop on the snowmobile trail, the Oxbow Inn offers gorgeous views of Oxbow Lake from the deck that should not be overlooked. Frequently open late, with great drink prices and an engaging crowd, the Oxbow Inn could easily be designated as the last stop on the trail. Mostly, though, it seems to be the hardest place to leave.

SOUTHERN & SACANDAGA

518.548.7551

SUMMER HOURS:

Monday - Tuesday
Open at 4 pm

Wednesday - Sunday
Open at 11:30 am

OFF-SEASON HOURS:

Wednesday - Sunday
Open at 11:30 am

CLOSED

**Two weeks in early spring
Two weeks at Thanksgiving**

HAPPY HOUR

*Summer only
Wednesday - Friday*
3 to 6 pm

Sport Island Pub

Another we will categorize as a resort bar, Sport Island Pub flaunts amenities beyond expectation. Located directly on Great Sacandaga Lake, just off Route 30 in Northville, it's a haven for winter and summer recreation. Sport Island, now underwater as a result of the Sacandaga dam, was once a resort playland similar to Coney Island. The railroad carried city visitors to the area and put them up in company-owned cottages, where they spent idyllic summers on the lake. A bridge from the mainland was constructed and dismantled every year, allowing vacationers access to a carousel, ball field, and carnival rides on the island.

Sport Island Pub's array of seating options presents a predicament. The vast, open floor plan in the bar and restaurant offers table seating near a crackling fire or in booths along the walls. The main bar accommodates at least 16 on comfortable padded stools. A little wandering reveals a continuation of the bar into a sunroom overlooking the lake. If sunshine and lake breezes are more your style, an outdoor deck holds more tables for dining or drinking with companions. A word of caution: Sport Island Pub's deck has a live webcam, with viewing from its website. If you prefer not to have your whereabouts made public, choose seating away from the carved bear. Several beachfront picnic tables supply informal seating by the lake. Another large room, with its own deck, is located upstairs for private parties.

The bar, of gleaming pine with overhead custom oak cabinetry, is the focal point of the room. The unfinished hardwood floor, wide rough pine walls, post-and-beam ceiling, and stone fireplace exhibit simple but striking rusticity. An antique brass draft tower dispenses eight varieties of beer and is an eye-catching nautical accent behind the bar. Bartenders are willing to conjure up a fancy cocktail, of their own invention or yours. Sport Island Pub has provided its signature Sand

SOUTHERN & SACANDAGA

518.863.2003

SUMMER HOURS:

Daily
Open at 11 am

OFF-SEASON HOURS:

Thursday
Open at 4 pm

Friday - Sunday
Open at 11 am

CLOSED

Major holidays
One week in April

HAPPY HOUR

Summer only
4 to 6 pm

Island Breeze recipe in the drink chapter.

If choosing seating seems a challenge, wait until you see the food. The menu lists a plethora of appetizers, soups, salads, burgers, specialty sandwiches, and gourmet pizzas. Pasta, chicken, fish, and steak dinners provide more substantial fare. Cajun chicken tortellini, fried smelt, and fried dough are among the more unusual choices.

Sport Island Pub is a summer and winter destination with a full calendar of activities. A Mexican Night special, Coors Lite drink specials, radio station hostings, ice races, and ice fishing are just a few of the attractions offered throughout the year. Musical entertainment is featured regularly on Saturday nights and Sunday afternoons in the summer. Fireworks displays are common during winter events, and become grander in scale for July 4th and Labor Day weekends.

Owner Anthony Lanzi is a gracious host who takes time to greet his customers as often as possible. The Lanzi family is now in its third generation in the restaurant business and is grooming the fourth. Anthony and his brother, Joseph, converted the former Beachcomber Bar and Restaurant into the Sport Island Pub in 1997. Lanzi's on the Lake, in nearby Mayfield, is owned and operated by two more Lanzi brothers, Lou and Larry, and Partners Pub and Grill in Johnstown is owned by brother Chris.

Sometimes a forgotten or overlooked region of the Adirondack Park, Great Sacandaga Lake patiently waits to be noticed. Unlike many of the resort towns of the park, this area is not overrun with great throngs of people and heavy traffic. The pace is more in line with what a vacation is supposed to be.

sportislandpub.com

Stony Creek Inn

The town of Stony Creek isn't the kind of place to be just passing through. Visitors either come here on purpose, or they're lost. Roads from Thurman, Warrensburg, Luzerne, and Wilcox Lake wilderness wearily converge at the "four corners" to take a rest. The Stony Creek Inn, roadhouse, honky-tonk, and restaurant, stands watch over this intersection as it has for over a century. Offering decent food, rudimentary lodging, and some of the finest music the area has to offer, the detour from mainstream destinations is worth the diversion.

Built in 1905 with locally milled lumber, before electricity made its way to Stony Creek, little has changed over the years. The hardwood floor is mostly concealed by layers of wax, blackened over the century. The only area of bare wood is the dance floor, worn too thin by countless dancing feet to sand it even one more time. The front porch offers a place to escape the din, cool off after bumping bodies on the dance floor, have a conversation, or just hear yourself think. Hunters and outdoor enthusiasts often inhabit the upstairs rooms, rented nightly for $35. A step above camping, the accommodations offer no cell phone reception, no TVs, or even room keys, but clean sheets and plenty of hot water in the communal bathroom.

What the inn lacks in ambience is compensated with enthusiasm and individuality. Yuppies and hippies, bikers and beatniks, artists, musicians, professionals (buttoned-down and buttoned-up), intellectuals, and vacationers of all ages populate the inn throughout its season. Weekdays promise a quiet dinner crowd and local bar population, but to truly experience the Stony Creek Inn, weekends are the best time to visit. Owners Dot and John have built upon the inn's musical roots and take pride in its entertainment lineup. Once home to bluegrass pickers, fiddlers, and square dancing, the inn continues its tradition with world-class musicians as diverse as its patrons. The Stony Creek Band, an Adirondack icon for 40 years, always packs the

HAPPY HOUR IN THE HIGH PEAKS

6 Roaring Branch Road, Stony Creek

house and is a must-see attraction.

Community spirit is displayed through the collection of artwork, posters, photos, and memorabilia hanging on the walls. The beginning of the end of the season is heralded by the appearance of the Big Buck Contest chart over the bar, with participants from near and far. Among newspaper articles and vintage photographs of the Stony Creek Inn is an original poster, now framed and signed by local musicians, given in appreciation for Dot and Johnstock, one of many annual fundraisers hosted at the inn for such beneficiaries as Cindy's Cancer Retreat and the Southern Adirondack Musicians Fund. Featuring food, music, and a silent auction, you're bound to find a must-have among the locally donated auction items.

Dot Bartell and John Fickel, curators of this exhibit, have tended the inn for over 32 years. Dot can be spotted darting throughout the dining rooms, meeting, greeting, and seating diners. John is in the kitchen but makes frequent appearances, usually wearing a stained apron over shorts, and a bandanna on his head. Both toil endlessly in this labor of love that is the Stony Creek Inn.

Drinks (and bartenders) are straightforward. No fancy martinis or trendy shooters here. A limited variety of bottled and draft beers, simple mixed drinks, and the inn's signature margarita are the norm. With only two bartenders on a busy night, expect to wait awhile to quench your thirst. Just relax. Listen to the music. Look around.

Whether to lose yourself or find yourself, treat yourself to a picturesque drive to the Stony Creek Inn, where "the road to a friendly place is never long."

SOUTHERN & SACANDAGA

518.696.2394

SUMMER HOURS:

Thursday - Sunday
Open at noon

OFF-SEASON HOURS:

Thursday - Sunday
Open at noon

CLOSED

December - April

stonycreekinn.net

High Peaks Region

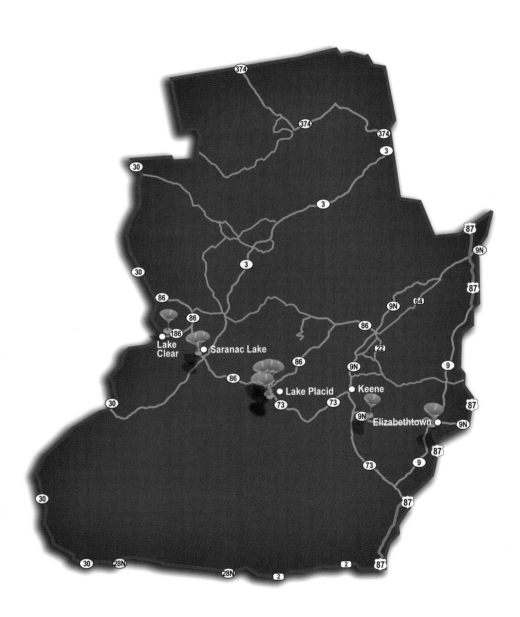

The Bars

Elizabethtown
- Cobble Hill Inn

Keene
- Baxter Mountain Tavern

Lake Clear
- Charlie's Inn

Lake Placid
- The Cottage at Mirror Lake Inn
- Lake Placid Pub & Brewery
- Liquids and Solids at the Handlebar
- Lisa G's
- Zig Zags Pub

Saranac Lake
- Captain Cook's Bar & Grill
- Grizle T's

HIGH PEAKS

Baxter Mountain Tavern

Recommended to us by numerous hikers, the Baxter Mountain Tavern was obviously well known to so many others—locals, seasonal residents, and tourists. Its location on Route 9N, between Elizabethtown and Keene, had eluded us. We'd traveled to Elizabethtown, then back, and had been through Keene numerous times on our way to Lake Placid and beyond, but never connected the dots. One more reason to abandon the GPS and find your own way.

The single-story ranch structure, a study in tan and green, is simple and unassuming. Baxter Mountain Tavern has a large parking area with room for all. The deck area overlooks a view of a grassy hill giving way to tall pines and nearby mountains. Baxter's location in High Peaks central, quite close to Baxter and Hurricane trailheads, makes it a convenient place for an after-hike meal or beverage. Though defined as a tavern by name, it's better defined as a fine restaurant. Pine paneled walls, birch bark wall sections embellished with twigs, and a comfortable couch situated in front of a cozy fireplace suggest a tavern atmosphere, but the menu, the service, and the clientele exceed the expectations of the typical tavern.

With no WiFi, spotty cell service, and only one television, it's more a place to meet up with friends or make new acquaintances without those distractions. The bar, with its neat rows of ladder-back stools, is small and informal, conducive to meeting the neighbors. Except for the occasional use of first names, it was difficult to discern between locals and newcomers. One group shared a dish of calamari, indicating that they were acquainted with one another and that calamari was one of the specialties at Baxter's. The Baxter Mountain Tavern serves lunch and dinner, with entrees priced from $9 to $21. Food is served until 10 p.m. The menu, though not extensive, lists a variety of appetizers and entrees that stray from the typical Adirondack fare. Crab cakes, smoked trout, maple-glazed pork chops,

10050 NYS Route 9N, Keene

HIGH PEAKS

518.576.9990

SUMMER HOURS:
Daily
Open at 11 am

OFF-SEASON HOURS:
Daily
Open at 11 am

CLOSED
Major holidays

sesame-encrusted tuna, and even a few vegetarian entrees serve to tempt the palate. Enjoy dining in the "window room," on the patio, or at the bar.

An inspiring wine list and a half dozen draft beers, along with a somewhat reserved liquor selection, ensure that the visitor will find something drinkworthy. The Baxter's Tavern Bloody Mary is detailed in the recipe section. The wine list is an array of nearly 30 reds, whites, and champagnes, though all wines are welcome and carry a corking fee. Local and regional craft beers include Long Trail Ale, Switchback, Guinness, Blue Moon, Saranac Pale Ale, and Ubu—all solid and respectable. Drink prices are slightly high, though typical for the region and certainly not unreasonable. Happy Hour is not observed at the Baxter Mountain Tavern, but watch for occasional drink specials that pop up unexpectedly.

Formerly known as Murphy's Swiss Hill Lodge, the Baxter Mountain Tavern has been owned and operated by Dave and Hillary Deyo since 1998. Dave is a regular presence, greeting patrons and ensuring smooth operation. The tavern proudly supports local fundraising activities for the Keene Valley Fire Department, the Rod and Gun Club, a winter snowshoe tournament, and a variety of golf-based charities.

Whether passing by en route to further destinations, or making your descent from a nearby peak, the Baxter Mountain Tavern offers a friendly place to have a meal, share a snack, have a drink, and meet with friends. The Baxter Mountain Tavern does not offer live entertainment, but we're told the locals can be entertainment enough.

baxtermountaintavern.com

Captain Cook's Bar & Grill

L ocated on Broadway in Saranac Lake, Captain Cook's Bar & Grill is a community bar. A local bar is where people go when they have nothing better to do; a community bar is where they go to get things done. Captain Cook's is the headquarters for the Saranac Lake IPW—the Ice Palace Workers. Lifelong Saranac Lake resident Scott Cook has owned Captain Cook's since 2008. Extending his dedication beyond hosting the IPW, Scott and his three-year-old son joined the organization in the 2012–2013 winter season. Apparently, the IPW recruits them early to maximize lifetime support.

The uncomplicated exterior reveals little about what you'll find inside Captain Cook's Bar & Grill. The building itself dates back to 1888, but whatever nips and tucks have been done along the way make it look decades younger. Over the years, many tavern-keepers have hung their shingle over the door, with Shoes Bar & Grill and Back Door being the most recent. The bar can seat 14 to 16 people, but the room easily supports any size gathering. If the crowd gets too big, a dining area upstairs and an outdoor seating area off the bar can hold the overflow.

Though not easily discernible in the dim light, the top of the P-shaped bar is inlaid with topographical maps of the Adirondacks. High pine ceilings and walls accent the rustic birch-slab shelves. A 1934 Old Town canoe hanging on a far wall completes the Adirondack appeal. Several flags are tacked to the ceiling, and a large, bright-yellow model seaplane soars over the bar. Three flat-screen TVs are scattered about. No reference is found to the old Captain Cook—no ships, no sailors, no nautical theme. Canoe notwithstanding.

Captain Cook's features Happy Hour drink specials Monday through Friday, but the general prices are also reasonable. The standard pool table and electronic darts provide entertainment on quieter days. Live music is featured during Winter Carnival and sporadically during the year. Visit their website and Facebook page for

SUMMER HOURS:

Daily
Open at Noon

OFF-SEASON HOURS:

Daily
Open at Noon

HAPPY HOUR

Monday - Friday
4 to 7 pm

up-to-date specials and events. A small public parking area is adjacent to the bar, and on-street parking is just up the road and across the street.

Food is usually served until 10 p.m. The steady parade of take-out customers is an indication of the popularity of the chicken wings. The menu at Captain Cook's features several flavors of wings (including peanut butter), sandwiches, burgers, and hot dogs. Davidson Brothers "Captain Cook's IPA," Long Trail, Blue Light, and Samuel Adams seasonal make up some of the draft beer choices, which frequently change. Assorted flavored vodkas and Jagermeister suggest the bartenders may like to show some occasional creativity. Captain Cook's signature Roofie Coolata can be found in our recipe section.

The IPW meets regularly at Captain Cook's to plan and troubleshoot for the Saranac Lake Winter Carnival, and to celebrate victory afterward. After the winter carnival, the rugby team takes over Captain Cook's to prepare for the Can-Am Rugby Tournament. Held every summer, over 100 rugby teams converge on Saranac Lake to compete.

A community bar encourages variation in age, gender, interests, and occupation. Captain Cook's clientele are distinct in all categories, but are also some of the friendliest people in the Adirondacks. Given the great deal of work they do throughout the year, one wonders if the hospitality isn't part of the grand recruitment process.

If you're thinking of relocating to Saranac Lake, or just visiting, Captain Cook's is a great place to meet new people or to become part of the Saranac Lake community.

captaincooks.webs.com

Charlie's Inn

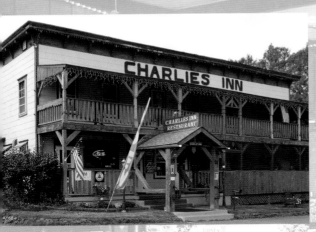

Escape the Great Camp style so overdone in the Adirondack Park and step into a true Adirondack bar at Charlie's Inn on Junction Road in Lake Clear. Dating back to 1891, when the Lake Clear Junction station was built, history of the common traveler permeates the pub. Walls cluttered with memorabilia from every decade of its existence represent those who have come before. Look past the lottery and snack vending machines and feel the echoes from the train station across the road. Imagine the rum runners making their way to and from Canada, stopping in to share stories, to eat, to rest, to engage in their commerce.

Jill Brockway and her husband, John, have owned the inn since 2008. John's family acquired Charlie's Inn in the 1990s, and kept the name the inn has carried for nearly 50 years. Jill manages the kitchen where menu options range from prime rib and haddock to wings and fried munchies. The dining room features wood floors, paneled walls in a waterfowl motif, a woodstove, and 1950s red vinyl and chrome chairs. A screened porch with deck furniture also provides additional seating—minus insects.

John's mother is still a frequent presence behind the bar. A quick glance at the drink specials menu, featuring the nouveau flavors of Dude or Bubble Gum vodka, may bring you from your reverie momentarily, but the drink prices are of days passed. Those trendy drink specials were obviously Jill's idea, because "Gram" (as Jill's mother-in-law prefers to be called) does not seem as savvy with them as she might a Rob Roy, Tom Collins, or draft beer, but a charming host nonetheless. Charlie's Inn's signature drink, Ecstasy Martini, is detailed in the recipe section. Beer variety is sufficient but unremarkable, with three drafts and nearly 20 bottles from which to choose. A daily Happy Hour includes complimentary hors d'oeuvres along with drink discounts.

Charlie's has all of the contemporary amenities we've come to expect like cell service, Quick Draw, several televisions, and even an ATM. But creature comforts like deer heads, stuffed birds, beaver, fox, and weasel will leave you feeling warm and fuzzy.

A 24-site campground on the property and seven rooms and a cabin for rent provide for a variety of companions coming and going, making it difficult to discern between visitors and locals. Charlie's regulars are known to describe Charlie's Inn as "a national treasure" and "simply real."

The campground and frequent outdoor events draw visitors during the summer. On the weekend following July 4th, Charlie's Inn hosts the annual Lake Clear Day, celebrating over 100 years of train station history. Charlie's Inn is a sponsor of local fundraising events like Life Flight, a biker poker run to support the local food pantry. Charlie's caters weddings on the vast and secluded grounds and puts on an occasional pig roast for charity.

Its location at the crossroads of several snowmobile trails makes Charlie's Inn a favorite spot among winter visitors on snowmobiles. An annual snowmobile poker run is held to support a variety of needy causes. Serving to enhance popularity with snowmobilers, Charlie's offers 24-hour access to gasoline.

Charlie's Inn is a welcome change from the overly competitive bars and taverns trying hard to stand out, and charging high prices for their uniqueness. Here you'll find a friendly greeting and a homey atmosphere on a working person's budget. Beware the little man carrying a book. He can trick you into buying him a drink, but it's worth the price to be engaged in the con.

HIGH PEAKS

518.891.9858

SUMMER HOURS:

Sunday
Open at noon

Wednesday - Saturday
Open at 11 am

OFF-SEASON HOURS:

Sunday
Open at noon

Tuesday - Saturday
Open at 11 am

CLOSED

Major holidays
Last week in March thru first week in April

HAPPY HOUR

Daily
4 to 6 pm

charlies-inn.com

Cobble Hill Inn

The Cobble Hill Inn, on Route 9 in Elizabethtown, is a bar, restaurant, and motel, owned by the Cashin family since 1991, and by Christina (Chrissy) Cashin, since 2006. Shamrocks on the imposing green chimney and stained glass window on the entrance door imply an Irish influence. Inside, a ceiling painted the color of a shamrock shake and maps of Ireland confirm those suspicions.

Yankees bobbleheads, banners, photos, and memorabilia are everywhere, leaving no doubt as to the allegiance of Cobble Hill's fan base. We'll leave it up to you if you want to root for some other team. The owners are proud of the family business and show community support by hosting a toy drive and other fundraisers throughout the year. Trophies and photos highlight the accomplishments of the inn's Monday night dart league. Mixed in here and there, Irish memorabilia complete the picture of the Cashin family passions.

The bar seats 10 and additional tables allow seating for 16 more. Baseball season guarantees that a Yankee game will be on one of the two TVs in the tavern area. Darts and Quick Draw are the only gaming amusements within the barroom. The pool table is located in the dining room. Musical entertainment is frequent on Friday and Saturday nights. Cobble Hill Inn even has its own song, "Cobble Hill Wobble," aptly written by Adirondack legend Mark Piper.

Chalkboard menus hang over the bar, announcing daily dine-in meal deals and beer specials like Yuengs and Wings or Pizza and a Pitcher. Comfort foods, such as chicken and biscuits or pasta alfredo, are found on the monthly specials menu. Quesadillas compete with burgers for top billing at the bar. Whether dining in or ordering take-out, food is served until 9 p.m.

An adjoining dining room gives distance and sanctuary from the bar. Tables cozy up to one of two fireplaces. An old upright piano

7432 Route 9, Elizabethtown

HIGH PEAKS

518.873.6809

SUMMER HOURS:

Wednesday - Monday
Open at 11:30 am

OFF-SEASON HOURS:

Wednesday - Monday
Open at 11:30 am

CLOSED

Christmas Day

HAPPY HOUR

Daily
4 to 7 pm

waits expectantly on a far wall, and an ancient phone booth in a corner provides solitude and privacy for cell-phone calls.

A proper assortment of liquors will satisfy most needs, and at very sensible prices, but frozen drinks are not an option at Cobble Hill. The signature Long Island Peach appears in the drink chapter. With 18 draft choices of domestic, Canadian, and a few regional craft brews, most drinks at Cobble Hill come from a tap and range from $2.50 to $7. A few bottled beer brands remain, but are rarely called for. Cobble Hill places an emphasis on clean draft lines, so no need to worry about swill in your swill.

An oversized parking area stands ready for the next big event, be it a pig roast, indoor or outdoor musical entertainment, or any spontaneous party. A deck along the side of the building holds chairs, benches, and tables for outdoor seating in the summer. A large awning provides shelter from rain and sun when venturing outside. The motel operates year-round, with four efficiencies and a total of seven rooms.

The Cobble Hill Inn is an amiable bar with attentive and engaging staff. Patrons are polite and outgoing, obviously comfortable sharing their favorite pub. Elizabethtown is the Essex County seat and gateway to the Adirondack High Peaks. If you're in town for jury duty or a traffic infraction, stop at the Cobble Hill Inn after for an empathetic ear to wash down your beer. If you're lost, stop in for directions. Any time of year, whether you're skiing, golfing, leaf peeping, or motorcycling in the area, you must drop in and make some new friends. The Cobble Hill Inn *is* the social life for the mostly local crowd.

cobblehillinn.com

The Cottage at Mirror Lake Inn

The Cottage is tucked on the edge of Mirror Lake, across from the Mirror Lake Inn in Lake Placid. Ed Weibrecht has owned and operated The Cottage since 1976, one of the longest runs of bar ownership in Lake Placid. Aging gracefully, The Cottage's multiple personalities are exhibited here, depending on the season and the time of day.

Winter is really what Lake Placid is all about. The tiny village hosted the 1932 and 1980 Olympic Winter Games. Whiteface Mountain, the fifth highest peak in the Adirondacks, is home to the greatest vertical drop east of the Rockies. Located in Wilmington, Whiteface is just a short drive from Lake Placid. For the cross-country skier or snowshoer, Mt. Van Hoevenberg is also minutes away. The Olympic Sports Complex attracts competitors and amateurs to its combination bobsled, luge, and skeleton track.

Summers in Lake Placid bring arts festivals, cycling events, horse shows, golfing, and scenic outdoor adventures. The Cottage attracts spectators, participants, seasonal residents, and visitors looking for an escape from sultry afternoons. The deck is comfortable, spacious, and reminiscent of the gardens of Avonlea. A neat, white fence and abundant plantings offer some privacy from the street. Lamps of wrought iron and blown glass hang from sturdy white posts. Indoors or out, the vantage point of The Cottage affords some of the best views of Mirror Lake and the surrounding mountains.

As the dinner crowd diminishes, the bar merriment begins. Happy Hour gets a late start at The Cottage, accommodating those unable to enjoy earlier happy hours around Lake Placid. Here the patrons gather after the day's work or adventures to share stories or connect with friends. The barstool offers sociability not found at a table. The bar at The Cottage seats only eight, but the half-wall partition provides a place to lean or set your drink and be part of the experience. The deck becomes more animated after dark, with more flexibility to move around.

77 Mirror Lake Drive, Lake Placid

Happy Hour starts at 9 p.m. with $3 draft beers and $4 margaritas or house wines. Taco Tuesday, offered from September to June, includes complimentary tacos and $4 margaritas from 5 to 7 p.m. During the winter, The Cottage holds an Apres Ski party every Wednesday from 4 to 6 p.m., with munchies and $3 drafts. Saturday night musical entertainment is provided monthly throughout the year, and weekly in the summer.

Specialty drinks are common at The Cottage. The most popular drink might be the bloody mary, served in a Mason jar mug. Build your own bloody mary by selecting your favorite vodka brand or flavor like Citron, Peppar, or cucumber, and garnish with classic celery; or take it up a notch with pickles, olives, pickled green beans, or shrimp. Margaritas, especially when available at $4, could easily take second place. If those aren't to your taste, the talent at the bar is sure to find something to please. A selection of domestic and imported bottled beers and eight quality drafts provides something for every beer drinker's preference.

Menu selections include appetizers, salads, hot and cold sandwiches, and desserts, served from 11:30 a.m. until 10 p.m. daily. The Cottage's appetizers, like baked brie, hummus, and spinach and artichoke dip, are more distinctive than pub food. Prices are in the above-average range, but the salads and sandwiches are tarted up in style.

Find solace by day or camaraderie by night. Be alone in the crowd or part of the crowd. No matter what you're looking for, The Cottage at Mirror Lake Inn has a mysterious way of becoming what you want it to be.

SUMMER HOURS:

Daily
Open at 11:30 am

OFF-SEASON HOURS:

Daily
Open at 11:30 am

HAPPY HOUR

Daily
9 to 11 pm

mirrorlakeinn.com

Grizle T's

A small sign hangs over the door of Grizle T's, barely visible from the street. Nestled between a pizza parlor and a café on Main Street in Saranac Lake, Grizle T's location is as obscure as its name. Owned by Adam Harris since 2007, Grizle T's is right on track as an entertaining and welcoming place to go.

No particular style of décor exists in the long, narrow interior, but Grizle T's has a homey, lived-in feel, like a family rec room, complete with five TVs (and NFL Sunday Ticket), foosball, darts, and a pool table. Various columns support the low, beamed ceiling, and beer art and photo collages plaster the walls. The wide-plank wood floor displays years of wear and a total disregard for the concept of level, but bears a strong sense of purpose.

The bar is a cool respite on a summer day and a warm relief in the winter. Several different areas offer additional seating away from the bar, with pub tables at the front and video gaming area at the rear. A deck off the back permits outdoor seating with built-in benches and several picnic tables, and allows smoking. A babbling brook below the deck provides free mood enhancement, but is meant to be enjoyed responsibly.

No formal Happy Hour is required here. Grizle T's clever daily drink specials have it covered. Extending your weekend, Micro Monday offers all-day mini-pitchers of domestic beer for $4, or microbrew at $6 to $7. On TwoFer Tuesdays, get two drafts or well drinks for the price of one, 9 p.m. to close. Whisky Wednesday means $2.50 house whiskey drinks and house choice draft all day. Thirsty Thursday entails two-for-one Harpoon IPA drafts all day. Grizle T's is the home of the 100-ounce challenge, all day, every day. Drink 100 ounces of beer in one hour, served 10 ounces at a time, then stumble

HAPPY HOUR IN THE HIGH PEAKS

53 Main Street, Saranac Lake

HIGH PEAKS

518.891.6393

SUMMER HOURS:

Daily
Open at 2 pm

OFF-SEASON HOURS:

Daily
Open at 2 pm

CLOSED

One week in April

away with a free t-shirt and your name affixed on the "wall of shame."

For the non-beer drinker looking for a challenge, the Fish Bowl is a rum-based drink served in a large fish bowl. It is *intended* to be shared. Typically, it comes with straws, but glasses are available for the feeble drinker. This one is for your own personal achievement—no glamorous prizes or recognition are bestowed. Finally, Mug Club members become Grizle T's regulars with oversized drafts served in a locally handmade mug.

Games are available on loan and include backgammon, Guess Who, Scattergories, and Phase 10. For techno-savvy players, try Nintendo ("old school" or Super) in the back room. There is something about playing a game while you're out at a bar that helps keep you focused and alert, not to mention just how much fun it is, and a great way to meet people. Be sure to stop by the photo booth to commemorate your visit. Occasional musical entertainment options are comprised of DJ karaoke or live music.

Grizle T's microwave menu might suffice in a pinch, but the pizza shop next door has its own walk-up window into the bar to take and deliver orders. WiFi is available at Grizle T's, and an ATM is on the premises. In an effort to appease the graffiti artist in most of us, the bathroom walls are covered in chalkboard wallpaper. We left our URL, but were sure to wash our hands afterward.

Clientele consists of students, transplants, and summer tourists, ranging in age from mid-20s to late 40s. If you're older than 40 and think you're too old to party, bring your "inner 20-something." You know you have one.

Lake Placid Pub & Brewery

The Lake Placid Pub & Brewery, icon of North Country brewers and birthplace of Ubu Ale, is an interesting combination of three pubs. Like varieties of ale, each has a personality of its own to pair with mood or preference.

On the first level is PJ O'Neill's. Opening with the only Happy Hour among the three pubs, from 3:30 to 6 p.m., this venue is a self-proclaimed "true Irish pub" and prides itself on its status as the only "local pub" in Lake Placid. Smooth and rich in character, like a porter or stout, PJ O'Neill's is a complementary contrast to the upper levels, but with similar taste—lots of wood and brick and a stained-glass backdrop behind the bar. Serving the same fine Lake Placid brews that are available upstairs, PJ's is the place to go for a game of pool or just to hang out until 2 a.m.

Ascend the wide wooden staircase, illuminated by stained-glass windows, to the Lake Placid Pub on the second floor. Like its Ubu Ale—flavorful, colorful, and versatile—the pub suits a variety of tastes. Vintage posters, college pennants, and the brewery's collection of awards and medals decorate the pine walls. Numbered beer steins dangle over the bar, mouths expectantly agape. Fittingly, the signature drink at this bar is the Sampler, consisting of four-ounce pours of six of the brewery's house beers.

One more flight of stairs leads to the newest addition, the Hop Loft. Like an IPA—contemporary, complex, and fresh—the Hop Loft is at once bold and delicate, easily paired with dinner or a quiet gathering. Equipped to handle seating for 80, several rooms are partitioned to allow private parties or large groups. Nine leather-topped barstools characterize the simplicity of this classy bar. The Hop Loft is open daily through the summer, and Thursday through Sunday off-season. Be sure to visit the gift shop on this floor for Lake

813 Mirror Lake Drive, Lake Placid

Placid Pub & Brewery memorabilia.

Founded by Chris Ericson in 1996, the Lake Placid Craft Brewing Company soon found itself unable to keep up with growing demand. The brewery has expanded several times, finally entering into a partnership with the Matt Brewing Company, where most of its beer is now brewed and packaged for distribution all over the northeast. Brewing of small batches is still carried out on the premises, overseen by head brewer Kevin Litchfield.

The on-site brewery still produces at nearly full capacity. Windows in the Lake Placid Pub allow a glimpse into the small brewery where fermenters, bellies full, smugly withhold their amber elixirs until perfection is at its peak. The Lake Placid Brewery is the winner of several awards. Among the many: best brewery in New York State in 2005 and 2007, and best brewery in the Hudson Valley in 2003, 2005, and 2007 by the TAP New York Beer Festival.

A tempting variety of freshly brewed beers changes throughout the year and may be purchased on site, by the six-pack or the growler. The menu includes typical and atypical pub food with burgers, barbeque, sandwiches, and pub classics, most in the $10 range. A quick glance at the menu implies that much beer is spilled in the kitchen, and some lands in the pots. Look for beer-inspired sauces, dressings, soups, and locally baked Ubu breads.

Regardless of which pub or pubs you choose to visit at the Lake Placid Pub & Brewery, you'll find one of the finest selections of tasty brews in the Adirondacks. This is a not-to-be-missed attraction in Lake Placid.

SUMMER HOURS:

Sunday
Open at noon

Monday - Saturday
Open at 11:30 am

OFF-SEASON HOURS:

Sunday
Open at noon

Monday - Saturday
Open at 11:30 am

HAPPY HOUR

Daily
3:30 to 6 pm
at PJ O'Neill's

ubuale.com

Liquids and Solids at the Handlebar

L iquids and Solids at the Handlebar in Lake Placid is situated on the former site of a bar called The Handlebar. Though the new business began as Liquids and Solids in 2010, so many locals tacked on the description "at the Handlebar" that the new owners embraced it and took it as their own. Keegan Konkowski and chef Tim Loomis have kept the name, but otherwise transformed a local dive into a gastropub. The two have changed the composition of the bar and restaurant into a culinary science.

Pendants, with bare bulbs painted dark, hang over the bar, casting a mysterious light. Eggplant-colored walls showcase intriguing artwork. Random details add a tasteful touch of fancy to the simple shapes and spare ornamentation in the dining area. Plants and fresh flowers pop their lively heads from artfully labeled beer bottles. Beer and wine menus, handwritten in wide black marker on large paper grocery bags, hang pinched onto clipboards behind the bar. The room is cozy, with pub tables near the bar and standard tables toward the back. They offer privacy in their sparseness and an opportunity to enjoy the varied artwork on the walls.

The liquids are a deluge of cocktail and craft-beer-driven potables. More than 20 red, white, and sparkling wines from France, Chile, Argentina, Italy, South Africa, Australia, and California are listed at $7 to $10 a glass and $28 to $45 a bottle. The cocktail menu features more than a dozen lively and imaginative specialties, priced between $8 and $12, enlisting creative elements from spices and fresh herbs to lavender syrup and vinegar. Painstakingly prepared with many homemade ingredients, the potent concoctions include the Cilantro Daiquiri, Smoked Ale, Guava Margarita with a lime sugar rim, and the Balsamic Fizz, tantalizingly embellished with basil and balsamic vinegar. The Rum and Raisin is a cocktail of generous proportions made from The Kraken Black Spiced Rum, lime juice, raisin clove apple juice, and orange and pineapple juice, garnished

HIGH PEAKS

518.837.5012

SUMMER HOURS:

Tuesday - Sunday
Open at 4 pm

OFF-SEASON HOURS:

Tuesday - Saturday
Open at 4 pm

CLOSED

**Major holidays
Memorial Day weekend**

with raisins and an orange slice. At $10, it's a liquid light lunch unto itself.

The beer, a periodic table of sorts, consists of six drafts, several cans, and over 100 bottles in various serving sizes. There are 22 IPAs alone! Also, a dozen or so Belgian strong ales, a bevy of stouts, and a multitude of others—trappists, triples, porters, reds, browns, lagers, saisons, Italians, and Belgians to list just a few. Keeping up with the latest trend, draft beer is served in an over-sized wine glass at Liquids and Solids. Draft and bottled prices vary from $3.50 to $27.

The solids are full of constantly changing culinary surprises formulated with homemade sauces, purees, stocks, and syrups using whatever the local farmers have to offer. Making nearly everything themselves and using locally produced ingredients allows Keegan and Tim to keep their prices down. Utilizing mostly small plates of such ambitious offerings as charcuterie, ratatouille, barbecued sweetbreads, fried pork liver, polenta, and saffron cavatelli, the restaurant offers a handful of full-sized entrees and some daily specials at fairly small prices.

The dessert menu, equally captivating, is short and sweet. Finish with sweet potato pie, chocolate bacon pot de crème, or maple marshmallow and graham cracker tart. For the late-night diner, the kitchen is open until 11 p.m. Tables on a patio in front receive service from the bar and restaurant when weather permits.

The creative juices are flowing at Liquids and Solids. In both menu and venue, enjoy the whimsy that the name invokes. The liquids and solids are covered—the gases are up to you.

liquidsandsolids.com

Lisa G's

If you've ever met Lisa G., you know why you have to visit Lisa G's in Lake Placid. Her energy is in force everywhere. Don't worry about the calories in what you eat or drink—she'll burn them off for you. Lisa Grigoriadis has owned and managed Lisa G's since 1990. After so many years, it looks like she's learned everything except how to slow down. Fortunately, she's hired staff that can keep up with her, and they're smart and funny just like she is.

Variety and creativity, sprinkled with intelligence and a sense of humor, pervade the entire experience, from Lisa G's fun and quirky website to the tongue-in-cheek menu descriptions. Tastefully furnished with craftsman-style tables and stools, the pub at Lisa G's has an upscale but relaxed and eclectic feel enhanced by several original paintings whose bold and sometimes garish colors seem influenced by both Matisse and Toulouse-Lautrec. The long, cherry bar, softly illuminated by pendants, is spacious and appealing. A sitting area of plump, stuffed furniture and a patterned carpet soften some of the edginess within the burgundy-painted walls. A pool table in the back is out of character with the rest of the room, but asserts itself nonetheless.

If you're looking for a little less energy, the deck may be the safest spot. There is a bright and airy multi-level deck out back with mixed pub table and standard table seating. Natural still lifes, sometimes in motion, are framed by the curtained background of the deck.

No official Happy Hour is observed at Lisa G's, but Lisa keeps an arsenal of affordable beverages available daily. Several specialty drinks, most priced at $7 to $8, tempt the adventurous. One among her staff likened drink preparation to accessorizing. "It's all about the accessories, like the shoes or the purse."

Less exciting, but equally important, a bold compilation of wines,

6125 Sentinel Road, Lake Placid

drafts, and bottled beers beckon the more conventional. The draft beer offerings are in continual flux, but designed to satisfy most beer lovers. Utica Club and PBR in cans are available for those with even simpler palates. Margarita variations include the Lychee Margarita and the Mango Margarita (more mango than 'rita) with a cinnamon rim. Lisa has shared her signature Grapefruit Cooler in our recipe section.

The lunch and dinner menus offer a mouth-watering variety at a moderate cost. Lisa G's little bit of Greek goes a long way on the menu. Lunch options include appetizers, salads, eggplant parmesan, sandwiches, and burgers that are available until the kitchen closes at 11 p.m. most days. Dinner is served from 5 to 9 p.m. on Sunday, and from 5 to 10 p.m. otherwise. The dinner menu covers it all: pizza, shrimp, pork, chicken, fish, and even meatloaf.

The food, the drink, the clientele, and the bartenders are the major forms of entertainment at Lisa G's. Local residents mix well with tourists here. Conversations are inevitable between the two. With an atmosphere that befits the '30s and '40s eras, the pool table seems ready for a dapper pool shark carrying his own custom cue in its proper case. Classic cocktails like the Tom & Jerry or the Ginger Rogers are in keeping with the nostalgic air, but the Bloody Caesar might be the most popular performer year-round.

Whether visiting for food or drink or both, take a seat at the bar to feel your surroundings and get to know the staff and the customers, and maybe even meet Lisa G. herself. No matter the number of pubs you visit in Lake Placid, Lisa G's will make an impression.

HIGH PEAKS

518.523.2093

SUMMER HOURS:
Wednesday - Monday
Open at 11:30 am

OFF-SEASON HOURS:
Wednesday - Monday
Open at 11:30 am

CLOSED
Major holidays
May 1–10

lisags.com

Zig Zags Pub

Zig Zags Pub, on Main Street in Lake Placid, is a sports enthusiast's bar where competitors and spectators are equally welcome—you can't have one without the other. The theme is one of Olympic conquest, but every athlete's achievement is revered. Those who gather at Zig Zags are competitive by nature, and apply themselves to drinking with similar zeal. The work-hard/play-hard mentality is sacred here.

When planning your stay in Lake Placid, be sure your accommodations are within comfortable walking (or weaving) distance from Zig Zags Pub. Though you may be tempted to stop in as you first pass the trademark sporty red bobsled parked on the sidewalk, it is an experience best saved for last.

Zig Zags is named for curves 13 and 14 on the bobsled run. Numerous posters, photos, signs, and memorabilia support the predominant theme. A map of the world covers most of one wall, welcoming those who have visited from all over the globe. Brett Bousquet and Dave Sheffield have owned the pub since 1997. Brett is frequently found behind the bar, bantering with regulars who've settled in, while at the same time greeting and serving new arrivals.

Zig Zags is the only "true" bar in Lake Placid. Defined as a retail business establishment serving only alcoholic drinks for consumption on the premises, this is a classic bar with all the standard trimmings. Except during Happy Hour, no food is served here—one good reason to save this place for last. Besides, with so many great places to eat in Lake Placid, there's no need to go hungry.

The long bar with wooden stools can comfortably handle nearly two dozen patrons, but standing room comes naturally here. For the competitor, a pool table, darts (both traditional and electronic), foosball, and a few video games are scattered around the room. For the spectator, several pub tables occupy the windows overlooking Main Street. Various shelves here and there allow a place to set your

HIGH PEAKS

518.523.8221

SUMMER HOURS:
Daily
Open at 3 pm

OFF-SEASON HOURS:
Daily
Open at 3 pm

CLOSED
Major holidays

HAPPY HOUR

Monday - Friday
3 to 6 pm

drink while playing a game or conversing with others.

Zig Zags is open until 3 a.m. as long as local law permits. Even if late nights aren't your style, there's something about Lake Placid's fresh air and high altitude that makes the time pass very quickly. After meandering the village shops, having a cocktail here and there, and maybe dinner, day turns swiftly to night. When all of the other pubs in town have closed, Zig Zags is just getting started. Local employees and business owners wander in to shake off the day's stress. As training sessions conclude, athletes' endorphin levels are high, their competitive edge piqued. Competition of another sort begins.

The beer list is top-notch. More than 20 domestic and craft drafts and bottles will leave no thirst unquenched. A standard liquor selection holds a few surprises from Lake Placid's own craft distillery, Lake Placid Spirits.

Happy Hour is offered Monday through Friday from 3 to 6 p.m., with varying specials and complimentary hors d'oeuvres. Drink prices are very reasonable around the clock, so don't worry if you miss the designated Happy Hour. Weekly late-night specials include discounted beers on Blue Monday, Wicked Wednesday, and Thirsty Thursday. Live music plays on Friday and Saturday nights in the summer and on Saturday night in the winter. Visit their Facebook page for upcoming performances.

Zig Zags has a come as you are, I am what I am, laid-back and fun personality. The impression is one of a locals' hangout that likes to have company. Whether competitor or spectator, you'll make friends at Zig Zags.

Western Wilderness Region

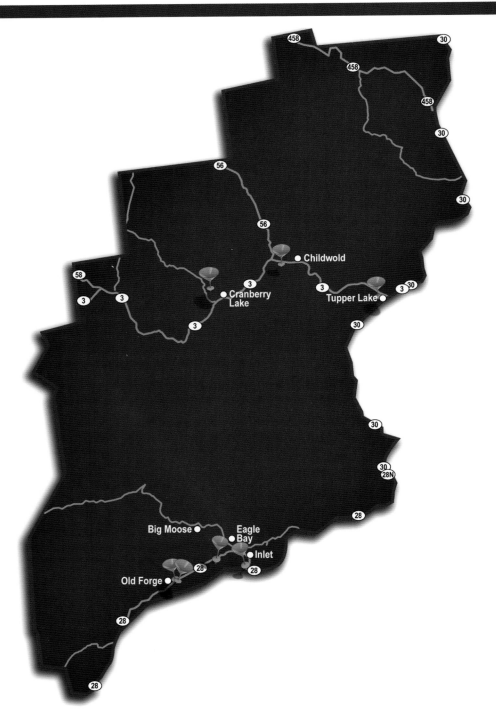

The Bars

Childwold
- Thirsty Moose Pub & Grub

Cranberry Lake
- Windfall Bar & Grill

Eagle Bay
- Big Moose Inn & Restaurant

Inlet
- Matt's Draft House at Screamen Eagle

Old Forge
- Daiker's
- Tony Harper's Too
- TOW Bar Inn

Tupper Lake
- P-2's Irish Pub

WESTERN WILDERNESS

Big Moose Inn & Restaurant

The Big Moose Inn & Restaurant is located directly on Big Moose Lake in Eagle Bay. Quiet and secluded, the Big Moose Inn has an air of simple sophistication and Adirondack lore. The covered porch, dotted with rocking chairs and expanding outward to a vast open deck overlooking the lake, inspires a feeling reminiscent of lazy summer vacations of years past. Several small docks on Big Moose Lake capture attention, drawing interest along an expanse of lawn to the lake and small beach. The Big Moose Inn's timelessness captures the imagination. A novelist could come here to spend a week and leave with a finished manuscript.

The tavern, cool and dark, with walls of wood and brick, complements the exterior charm. Visions of Ernest Hemingway entertaining friends in one of the booths, or John Irving alone at the bar, having strayed from his New England comfort zone, are easily conjured. Most eye-catching is the flutter of business cards that have alighted on the ceiling by the thousands like a rabble of migrating monarch butterflies. The tile ceiling is obscured by the cards, many yellowed after 30 years, skewered in place with straws, swizzle sticks, and cocktail picks. Despite criticism from state authorities, the current owner is compelled to leave them for their nostalgic significance. Can't blame him. We would leave them too.

Spotlights shine gently on the dark plank bar. Each of three booths on the opposite wall is illuminated overhead with a Tiffany-style lamp. A bright and cozy room with brick fireplace is tucked away beyond, and provides more private seating on high-backed slat benches.

Behind the bar, a display of flavored vodkas indicates that a better-than-average selection of drinks can be concocted here. The tavern lists a very nice collection of wines and several draft and bottled beers. Big Moose Inn has shared its Adirondack Martini, authentically made with 46 Peaks vodka and New York State maple syrup, in our recipe section.

1510 Big Moose Road, Eagle Bay

The tavern menu is comprised of appetizers, soups, salads, signature sandwiches, and hearty burgers. After 5 p.m., some dinner entrees are served in the tavern. The dining room menu expands with more steak, seafood, pasta, and house specialty entrees. Both the tavern and dining room menus are available until the kitchen closes at 9 p.m.

The inn, built in 1902 as an Adirondack camp, became known as the Big Moose Inn in 1946. Big Moose Lake has its own place in history as the location of the murder of Grace Brown by her lover, Chester Gillette, in 1906. Perhaps the most famous Adirondack ghost, stories of Grace Brown have inspired novels, a movie, and several non-fiction books. Even TV's *Unsolved Mysteries* produced an episode about Grace's ghost in 1996.

Mark and Susan Mayer have owned the Big Moose Inn since 2010. Obviously quite delighted with the inn, Mark will readily spend time with his guests, sharing stories on the history, trivia, hauntings, and his family's acquisition of the inn.

Winter and summer activities bring vacationers all year. The Big Moose Inn is on the Town of Webb snowmobile trail. Nearby, Inlet and Old Forge offer a number of events throughout the calendar. The inn, which is open year-round, has 16 uniquely decorated and named rooms. It's a great place for a family vacation, a romantic weekend for two, or a single retreat.

The Big Moose Inn isn't just for lodging guests. The tavern and restaurant invite people in for an afternoon or evening, too. Whether visiting long-term or short, it is sure to inspire your imagination.

WESTERN WILDERNESS

315.357.2042

SUMMER HOURS:

Saturday - Sunday
Open at noon

Monday - Friday
Open at 4 pm

OFF-SEASON HOURS:

Spring: Thursday - Sunday
Fall: Thursday - Tuesday
Winter: Monday - Thursday
Open at 4 pm

Winter: Friday - Sunday
Open at noon

CLOSED

Late March to early May
Late October thru
mid-December

HAPPY HOUR

Off-season only
Monday - Friday
4 to 6 pm

bigmooseinn.com

Daiker's

Daiker's, located on Fourth Lake in Old Forge, has universal appeal and ample space to amuse many. Whether entering from the large parking area or from the lake, it will take some time to take it all in. More than a restaurant and bar, Daiker's is an amusement park for adults.

The place is huge, more great hall than restaurant, with a lengthy bar that stretches outside onto the deck. A partition separates the bar from the dining area and has barstools for additional seating. Sports theme and rustic lodge engage in a unique interpretation of Adirondack style. A massive stone firepit commands the center of the room. Wildlife prints, displayed and for sale, hang on pine walls in the game room. Inflatable sports novelties hover among antler chandeliers suspended from log beams in the cathedral ceiling. In an alcove overhead, an Adirondack scene in diorama depicts a trapper's cabin, its tenant snoozing outside. Near the bar, a miniature of the original Daiker's bar is tucked among photos and signs. Vending machines, an arcade, a game room, and even a photo booth provide distractions beyond the customary. TVs and Quick Draw monitors are everywhere. Daiker's clothing line is on display and available for purchase. The bra collection, however, is not.

Daiker's is staffed with attention to demand. Both restaurant and bar can get very busy and the competent staff rise to the occasion. With a well-stocked bar, six drafts, and an abundance of bottled beers, there's something for everyone. Drinks are simple and designed with efficiency in mind. The bartenders are more attentive than friendly when the bar is full, but manage to smile and banter on the move. The menu includes appetizers, sandwiches, burgers, steaks, and dinner entrees. The restaurant serves food until 9 p.m., but the snack vending machine is open all night.

Originally called the Fulton House, Daiker's was once a casino and a stop for the steamboat that ran along the lake. Tal Daiker's dad bought the business in 1956 and it has been Daiker-family operated since then. In 1988, Tal and his wife, Debbie, took over operations, instituting changes, expansions, and improvements over the years. Their sons, Devin and Dane, also help with the family business, now in its third generation.

Daiker's is a popular venue during Old Forge's Winter Carnival in February, Snofest in March, and the Thunder in Old Forge motorcycle event in late May. Live entertainment is provided on Friday and Saturday nights in the winter, and on Wednesday, Friday, and Saturday nights in the summer. Sunday summer afternoons bring the addition of acoustic music on the deck, where you can enjoy a splendid view of Fourth Lake. Dogs are permitted on the deck, and water bowls are happily provided for these four-legged guests.

Daiker's takes full advantage of social networking, maintaining a website, a Facebook page, and two Twitter accounts. Follow DaikersOF for information on entertainment and events, and TalsTrailReport for updates on local snow conditions. Daiker's closes briefly in the spring and fall, so check the website before visiting off-season. Daiker's is six miles from the hamlet of Old Forge. However, MAC's Safe Ride, a non-profit group of volunteers, provides transportation from bars in Old Forge on weekends in exchange for a donation.

The clientele is extremely wide-ranging in age and interest at Daiker's. Boat shoes meet biker boots, snowmobilers melt into NASCAR and football fans, parents become couples at the cost of quarters for the arcade, young lovers sneak off to the photo booth for a clandestine kiss, and Five-Hour Energy rejuvenates retirees who stick around for late-night rock bands. Come play.

WESTERN WILDERNESS

315.369.6954

SUMMER HOURS:

Daily
Noon to 2 am

OFF-SEASON HOURS:

Monday, Wednesday, Thursday
Open at 4 pm

Friday - Sunday
Open at noon

CLOSED

Major holidays
Day after Labor Day

daikers.com

Matt's Draft House at Screamen Eagle

If trying to choose between 15 pizzas and 14 wings has you scratchin', try picking from 50 draft beers! Matt's Draft House is located inside the Screamen Eagle on Route 28 in Inlet. The Screamen Eagle is a family-owned complex comprised of a specialty pizza restaurant, video rental/gift shop, and the Draft House. The Screamen Eagle has been in business since 1993.

In 2006, remodeling was completed, creating a room in the back of the building for Matt Miller and Jonathan Miller to open Matt's Draft House. They began with eight drafts, an extensive selection of bottled beers, and a considerable wine list. In 2012, Matt's upgraded from 8 to 50 drafts, easily the largest assortment in the Adirondacks. While drafts dominate, bottled beers and wines are still available, but no poured liquors are served.

The draft lineup is comprised of commercially made domestics and imports, and domestic and imported craft brews. Several Belgian-style ales come from Ommegang Brewery in Cooperstown, New York. A few shandies traveled from the Leinenkugel Brewery in Chippewa Falls, Wisconsin. Originating in England centuries ago, a shandy is a beer mixed with juice or citrus soda, though the classic mix is with lemonade. Often compared to hard lemonade or a wine cooler, the shandy is favored as a refreshing summer drink. A few cider-based drafts are on tap for more variety.

Matt is frequently behind the bar, eager and willing to answer questions about the beers, make suggestions, and offer a sample. Expect a little ribbing when ordering a lite or ultra-lite beer at Matt's Draft House. Feel free to beat Matt to the punch line by asking for a Bud or Ultra "water."

The restaurant has a few tables for dining-in, but primarily serves take-out or patrons at the Draft House bar. As Matt's grows from draft

172 Route 28, Inlet

WESTERN WILDERNESS

315.357.6026

SUMMER HOURS:

Daily
Open at noon

OFF-SEASON HOURS:

Tuesday - Friday
Open at 3 pm

Saturday - Sunday
Open at noon

CLOSED

Major holidays

house to 8th Wonder of the World, at least among beer drinkers, changes in the floor plan are likely to occur. Currently the bar is standard in size, seating 12 to 14 people, with a few tables nearby. A deck overlooking the Inlet Channel provides more table and sidebar seating.

The town of Inlet is on Fourth Lake, part of the Fulton Chain of Lakes. Inlet is an attraction for swimming, boating, fishing, camping, and snowmobiling. The town center is small, even by Adirondack standards, but offers a number of things to do. For shopping, there are several gift shops, a general store that has it all, and even a bookstore. Arrowhead Park, in the center of Inlet, is located on the grounds of the former Arrowhead Hotel. A beach, playground, tennis courts, and boat docking are just some of the amenities. Arrowhead Park also holds concerts, art exhibits, and fireworks.

Matt's Draft House sponsors the local women's Screamers softball team in Inlet. In May, Matt's and the Screamen Eagle put on a pizza eating contest. Musical entertainment is common during the summer and for special events. Matt's has open WiFi, Quick Draw, an excellent patron-to-TV ratio, and lottery ticket vending in the restaurant area. A webcam on Matt's website provides snowmobile conditions in winter or party conditions in summer.

Matt's is a small bar with a busy restaurant. Once word is out, you may find you can't get in and have to order your pizza, wings, and a growler of your favorite beer on tap to go. To ensure you'll get in the next time you visit, you might want to keep the 50 beers on tap a secret.

mattsdrafthouse.com

P-2's Irish Pub

The brick building, trim and neat, stands just feet from the sidewalk on Main Street in Tupper Lake. P-2's Irish Pub's sign, illuminated in red and green neon, replaces its former moniker, Al's Lounge.

Inside, a suit of armor stands guard at the pool table, silently observing. Dimly lit with amber pendants and recessed spotlights, the interior's Irish pub characteristics gradually come to light. The curved bar, a rich, dark wood with red padded front, shows signs of its age and character. Old cigarette burns mar the top, scars of forgotten conversations and decades of good times. Arrow-back bar stools match the green faux-leather walls, padded for comfort or sanity. Tin ceiling, oak woodwork, and round, solid-oak pub tables surrounded by sturdy backless stools all add warmth and character to this charming space.

Al's Lounge was founded in 1966 by Joseph "P-2" LeBlanc, but its history dates back to 1949, when it was known as Ivan's Lounge. In 2006, it was acquired by Joseph's daughter, Michelle LeBlanc Blair, and revamped into P-2's Irish Pub, named in honor of her father.

It's a small pub but is able to handle any amount of activity. The full-size bar seats 10 to 12, and several pub tables await more guests, but P-2's still has room for a pool table and darts. A new patio is accessible from the side of the pub, expanding capacity and accenting the seating options with Patty O'Furniture. Watch for a new phenomenon in Tupper Lake as regular P-2's patrons show off their sunburns.

Two large-screen TVs are enough to follow your favorite game, but not be consumed by it. Collages and team photos attest to P-2's community spirit. They seem to sponsor a team for everything. P-2's frequently hosts private parties and holiday celebrations. Open WiFi is available to customers. An ATM is on site, possibly for Quick Draw enthusiasts, but credit cards are also accepted.

WESTERN WILDERNESS

518.359.9980

SUMMER HOURS:

Daily
Open at 2 pm

OFF-SEASON HOURS:

Tuesday - Saturday
Open at 4 pm

HAPPY HOUR

Daily
4 to 7 pm

Drink specials range from the signature Blue Margarita to a P-2's style Black & Tan, with spontaneous options in between. P-2's is the only establishment in town that serves Guinness on tap. In addition to drafts, an interesting array of bottled and canned beers assures quenching of the most discriminate thirst.

All of their food is rumored to be the best, but the chicken wings, chicken breast dippers, and sweet potato fries are favored among many of the patrons. Most menu items are affordably priced under $10.

The opening of the Franklin Dairy Music Hall, a converted barn located behind the pub, has allowed P-2's to expand into a premier music venue able to pack in larger crowds. The barn was home to the Franklin Dairy until the 1980s and had been used for storage. Following much restoration and renovation, P-2's held its first concert in 2012. Deemed a smashing success, the old dairy aroma was replaced with the essence of stale beer.

Music is a staple at P-2's, with open mic night at least once a month all year. You'll find the occasional Irish band, featured artists in the pub on weekends, the Outdoor Summer Music Series under the tent, and more in the works in the music hall. See their website or Facebook page for up-to-date listings.

Offering outstanding service, loyal and happy customers, friendly prices, and a musical hotspot, P-2's claim as "The Place to be in the Adirondacks" is an accurate assertion. At least in the Tupper Lake region. P-2's is a traditional neighborhood pub, more authentic than the typical "Irish pub" that flaunts its blarney.

p2sirishpub.com

Thirsty Moose Pub & Grub

The Thirsty Moose Pub & Grub is located on Route 3 in Childwold, somewhere between Cranberry Lake and Tupper Lake. The exterior is unremarkable, with obvious additions to what was once a simple home. The sign promises a restaurant and lodging, but the name implies something more.

In 2002, Mickey and Jan Sylvester bought and renamed the Thirsty Moose, formerly known as Dumas's. They have remodeled and upgraded inside and out. Five cabins are for rent behind the Thirsty Moose, and they too are kept up-to-date. Even the landscape appears to be an ongoing project, possibly an excuse for Mickey to use his heavy equipment for enhancement of the surrounding grounds.

A semicircle of dark mahogany or cherry, the handcrafted bar is the focal point of the room and perfectly conducive to conversation. The bar seats 12 to 14, but leave room for Mickey. The dining room, with its red tablecloths and neat white chairs, is in an adjoining room away from the bar. A menu of burgers, steaks, seafood, chicken, and more lists prices from $7.95 to $24.95. Bar nibbles of the mostly fried variety range from $2.50 to $11.95.

Though no formal Happy Hour designation exists, drink prices are very reasonable. Nearly 20 bottled beers are offered. Domestic is priced at $2.75, higher-end bottles are $3.50, and draft (Bud Light) is $2.25. Red and white wines are available for $4, and shots and mixed drinks vary in price. The Thirsty Moose Pub & Grub has shared their signature Washington Apple shot in our drink recipe section. Bartenders at the Thirsty Moose have a creative streak and enjoy introducing new drinks to unsuspecting guests. We liked the Tic Tac—orange vodka and Red Bull, each separately contained within a rocks glass filled with Red Bull (a bomber shot), but recommend going wherever the bartender's inspiration takes you.

In the rare event that the staff and clientele aren't amusement

SUMMER HOURS:

Friday - Sunday
Open at noon

Tuesday - Thursday
Open at 3 pm

OFF-SEASON HOURS:

Friday - Sunday
Open at noon

Tuesday - Thursday
Open at 3 pm

enough, Quick Draw and New York Lottery are on site along with a pool table, dartboard, and several televisions. A jukebox is stocked with non-disco music, mostly '70s rock, but sometimes enlists the accompaniment of the overhead disco ball. The ring game, best described as a ring on a string attached to the ceiling, challenges expert and novice to get the ring on the hook on an opposite wall. Those who have mastered it make it look easy. Remember, five cabins are available if you want to stick around until you master the game.

As a meeting place for so many, the Thirsty Moose amuses bikers, vacationers, hunters, snowmobilers, and, of course, everyday fun seekers. During the summer, it's an after-work gathering place for seasonal employees from as far away as Lake Placid. The Childwold Snowpackers meet at the Thirsty Moose monthly. You may find them there frequently throughout the winter, either planning or relaxing after grooming the nearby snowmobile trails.

For the thrill seeker, watch the crowd gather or the snow fall via the Snowpacker's web cam that monitors activity outside the Thirsty Moose. A sign out on the trail points the direction to the Thirsty Moose, promising "Bar, Food, Gas and Love." We can't attest to the gas, but we were feeling the love.

Mickey is a regular presence at the Thirsty Moose, honing and testing his rather dry humor on anyone who will play along. A For Sale sign is inconspicuously displayed outside, but we got the impression that Mickey would be hard-pressed to let it go. It seems his staff are more like family than employees, and his customers more like friends.

Tony Harper's Too

Located on Main Street in Old Forge, the unique exterior of Tony Harper's Too is hard to miss. Stone and brick, inside and out, a semi-circular façade extends the confines of the interior, invoking a sense of being outside while in, or vice versa. Looking up into the turret-like structure reveals a spoke-work ceiling of pine. An enormous metal chandelier hangs from its center. Inside, the three-sided bar, built of corrugated metal topped with a polished hardwood surface, continues outdoors, creating a breezy, open feel. Despite what the sign reads, this is not your typical pizza and clam shack.

The original Tony Harper's is a small roadside tiki bar in Raquette Lake, serving up good pizza and clams during the summer. What began as a hobby eventually grew into an enterprise. Owner Lisa Murphy enlisted the help of her husband's construction business to design a new building, restaurant, and bar in the heart of Old Forge. Most recently, Tony Harper's Too has added accommodations over the bar, where single rooms include a kitchenette and deluxe rooms have a full kitchen. Rooms are available by day, weekend, or longer. A fully furnished apartment is rented by the week or for a whole season.

Old Forge is a vacation destination. Summer visitors come for the plentiful lakes, hiking trails, and the Enchanted Forest/Water Safari amusement park. Many more tourists flock here in the winter for snowmobiling. Nearby, McCauley Mountain offers scenic chairlift rides in the fall and downhill and cross-country skiing in winter. Wandering in and out of the many shops in Old Forge is a year-round activity. Old Forge Hardware is a general store bordering on the extreme, selling toys, clothes, books, hardware, kitchenware, and so many oddities you didn't know you needed.

Tony Harper's Too has a rotating stock of draft beers, as the collection of semi-retired taps will attest, and many more in bottles. Standard mixed drinks can be readily prepared, but are kept simple

WESTERN WILDERNESS

315.369.3777

SUMMER HOURS:

Daily
Open at 11 am

OFF-SEASON HOURS:

Daily
Open at 11 am

during peak hours. Bartenders, frequently busy, strive to keep up with demand. From a relatively small workspace behind the bar, they're serving drinks for diners and bar guests, both inside and out.

Favorites from the menu are not limited to pizza and clams. Chicken wings and burgers are a necessity for many. Daily lunch specials introduce new and unique sandwiches or entrées. The kitchen remains open until 10 p.m. weekdays and until midnight or later on weekends, making Tony Harper's Too a popular late-night dining locale.

On weekend nights, live music is the main attraction at Tony Harper's Too, where crowds gather inside and out, some dancing informally wherever space permits. People mingle on the patio where they can hear one another and still hear the music. Tony Harper's Too has live entertainment on Thursday, Friday, and Saturday nights in the summer and only on Saturday nights in the off-season. Tony Harper's Facebook page is the best source for the music lineup.

An interesting mix of people gravitates to Tony Harper's Too. Locals hop from bar to bar, either seeking one another or out of fear of missing something. Like wandering trail guides looking for work, they are eager to make new acquaintances or share intel about Old Forge. Tourists come tempted by food or are lured by music, but everyone gets sucked into the party atmosphere. With music playing and boisterous crowds shouting to be heard over the din, everyone just keeps adding to the noise. Come for the music, but stay for the fun. Make some new friends or just make some noise.

tonyharperspizzaand
clamshack.com

TOW Bar Inn

The TOW Bar Inn, on Main Street in Old Forge, is a conventional bar without frills or fanfare. Some may be compelled to label it a dive bar, but it's really a local bar with only a few dive tendencies. And people love it. It's a curiosity.

A dive bar has only one bartender on duty, and he's old and cantankerous. There is nothing cantankerous about Jack. If you enter and find Jack (a.k.a. Jackson, Famous Jack, or Action Jackson) behind the bar, sit down, relax, and expect to enjoy yourself immensely. Jack, head mixologist, has been a fixture at the TOW Bar since 1990. Apparently, he came with the deed when the current owner, Andy Hopsicker, purchased the bar in 2007. Jack's fervent supporters, our TOW Bar buddies, strongly profess him to be "the best." We have witnessed Action Jackson in action. His patience is outstanding, but what stands out above all other qualities is his genuine friendliness. Imagine working in a bar for over 20 years and having any patience at all.

A dive bar reeks of stale beer and soggy cigarettes. Though there are some bars that still retain the odor of cigarettes after years of being smoke-free, the TOW Bar smells of fresh popcorn. On the subject of food, a dive bar sells potato chips, peanuts, and pickled eggs, but TOW Bar has free popcorn.

There are no fancy signature drinks, blenders, or drink umbrellas in a dive bar—it's strictly about the beer or the shot. TOW Bar's shelves are well stocked, and Jack will happily improvise if he doesn't have what you're looking for. It will be shaken or stirred and served in a simple glass, lipstick-stain free. TOW Bar's 20 or so bottled beers are unpretentious and mostly domestic. Drafts include LaBatt Blue, Blue Light, and Budweiser. A dive bar's pricing is rock bottom. TOW

3065 Main Street, Route 28, Old Forge

WESTERN WILDERNESS

315.369.6405

SUMMER HOURS:

Daily
Noon to 2 am

OFF-SEASON HOURS:

Daily
Noon to 2 am

CLOSED

Major holidays

CASH ONLY

Bar's is not quite.

The only accoutrements decorating a dive bar are neon beer signs and outdated liquor ads. In TOW Bar, Yankees, Giants, and NASCAR fans will feel comfortable among the bobbleheads, old photos, and autographed memorabilia. The works of Doug Green, house cartoonist, are exhibited throughout the TOW Bar. One is a cartoon of John Ratzenberger, Cliff Clavin of *Cheers* fame, who stopped in and played pool with some of the regulars. Sandra Bullock is listed among other famous visitors to the TOW Bar. It's a fact. Famous people don't frequent dive bars.

A real dive bar is open 365 days a year and stays open as late as laws permit. TOW Bar is closed for Thanksgiving and Christmas, and closes nightly at 2 a.m.

According to experts, a dive bar has at least one seat occupied by a creepy old drunk of indeterminate gender who shows up to claim that seat long before noon. The TOW Bar doesn't even open until noon, and has a cheering section of local Jackson fans who've taken over the creepy end of the bar. Working in shifts, they secretly update their stand-ins with stories about the strangers seated at the bar. They know what the TOW in TOW Bar stands for, and might even tell you. They are funny and nice. They are the TOW Bar buddies.

TOW Bar is home to the locals, but enjoys entertaining (verb as well as adjective) visitors. Next time you're in Old Forge, stop into the TOW Bar Inn to shoot some pool, play darts, eat some popcorn, or enjoy live entertainment on Sunday night. See for yourself why it's so popular. YOU try to explain it.

Windfall Bar & Grill

Look! Out in the woods … it's a bar … it's a restaurant … it's Windfall Bar & Grill! Just a few miles from the hamlet of Cranberry Lake, on Tooley Pond Road, the Windfall awaits.

The Windfall is located on a heavily trafficked snowmobile trail a few miles from Cranberry Lake, the third largest lake in the Adirondack Park. A dam built on the Oswegatchie River in the 1800s flooded the lake and doubled its size, but destroyed the once bountiful bogs. Perhaps because nearly 75 percent of the shoreline is state owned, or because only two points on the lake are accessible by road, the lake remains mostly serene.

Friendlier than a franchise restaurant…. John and Rosalyn Dragun have owned the Windfall Bar & Grill since 2006. According to Roz, they've taken it from rowdy reputation to an eating destination. Occupying a yellow ranch house, neither garish nor pretentious, it's a simple-looking country tavern and restaurant, well maintained and hospitable. The same is found within.

Windfall Bar & Grill has its share of amenities. Just inside the door, the pine bar comfortably seats 8 to 10, with two booths and a few tables for seating near the bar. Complete with its own upright piano and lighting, a small niche across the room supplies space for musical performers. Two TVs, a pool table, darts, Quick Draw, and lottery scratch games provide amusement, whether you're waiting for a table or having a drink.

More colorful than a cranberry merchant…. Creativity runs rampant in the kitchen, on the menu, and in the specialty drinks. A sense of humor permeates and has a tendency to be contagious. John is an expert in the field of layered shots. The Windfall features a number of cleverly named, delicious shots. The Jellyfish and Chastity Belt are popular with the crowds of snowmobilers who slide through the door every winter.

Windfall's lineup of draft and bottled beers is sufficient, revealing no surprises. Also on tap: Windfall Bar & Grill's house-made root beer. The wine list includes a house-made sangria, eight red, six white, and

550 Tooley Pond Road, Cranberry Lake

a sparkling wine, along with several house wines available by the glass or bottle. See the signature Windfall Punch in the recipe section.

A winter destination among snowmobilers, the Windfall holds its own in the summer with its solid restaurant reputation and attention to service. The Draguns are very selective in staffing, despite the limitations their location presents. Optimism perseveres in sluggish times.

Entertainment comes in the form of karaoke and an occasional acoustic band. During Presidents' weekend in February, they host a winter-weekend party with a chicken barbecue and live music. The St. Patrick's Day party tends to be the last hurrah for snowmobilers.

Able to please hungry tourists with a single meal…. John, co-owner and chef, is a graduate of the Culinary Institute of America in Hyde Park. The dining menu features the Windfall's signature chicken picatta, seafood dishes, steak, ribs, and a tempting dessert list. All can be enjoyed in the cozy but open dining room, with views of the landscape and local wildlife. Burgers, salads, sandwiches, and sides are listed on the pub menu, most priced from $4.99 to $9.99. John's own dijon horseradish salad dressing should be bottled and sold on the premises.

Visit the Windfall for the food, the warm hospitality, and occasional music. Enjoy the drive among the pines and ponds on this idyllic route down the road less traveled. Reservations are highly recommended, especially on the busiest days.

Fighting a never-ending battle for food, cocktails, and the American way! The Windfall Bar & Grill is just super, man.

WESTERN WILDERNESS

315.848.3559

SUMMER/WINTER HOURS:

Friday - Sunday
Open at noon

Wednesday - Thursday
Open at 3 pm

OFF-SEASON HOURS:

Thursday
Open at 3 pm

Friday - Sunday
Open at noon

CLOSED

Month of April
Week before Christmas

windfallbarandgrill.com

Trailheads

Selecting just 46 bars was much too difficult, so we chose another 46 that we call the Trailheads. This section lists the Trailheads, with brief highlights about each one. If you find yourself in the neighborhood of one of the Trailheads, don't hesitate to stop in.

Foothills

Ashe's Hotel
85 Hudson Street
Warrensburg
518.504.4355
One of the oldest, continuously operating bars in the Adirondacks. A townie bar, but a favorite stop for some. Popular venue for Americade and Bike Week. DJ or live music on weekends.
Open daily.

The Barking Spider
302 Main Street
North Creek
518.251.9911
Meeting place for skiers and outdoor adventurers. Closest thing to a local bar in North Creek. Limited menu served from 6 to 11 p.m. Locals are more like guides and staff is super.
Open daily.

Bear Trap Inn
107 West Main Street
Indian Lake
518.648.5341
Primarily a biker bar, but all are welcome—just bring an open mind. Drink choices are minimal, and so are the prices. Bar is tiny, with a separate dining area.
Open daily.

Black Bear Restaurant
7901 State Route 9
Pottersville
518.494.9972
Popular local bar with standard pub food, pool table, and a loyal fan base. Bottled beer and simple mixed drinks are priced right.
Open daily.

Black Mountain Lodge
2999 State Route 8
Johnsburg
518.251.2800
Bar easily morphs between service bar and tavern for locals, Gore Mountain skiers, and tourists. Family-friendly restaurant and lodge with 25 rooms.
Bar open daily.

Flanagan's Pub
1075 US Route 9
Schroon Lake
518.532.9096
Adirondack-country motif. Nicely maintained bar and restaurant.

Drink specials during the
summer months.
Open year-round.

J & J Foxx Lair Tavern
2467 State Route 28
Bakers Mills
518.251.0133
Biker bar; local hangout.
Basic drink options at
low prices. Occasional
entertainment brings variety to
the usual crowd.
Open year-round.

Newcomb House
5699 State Route 28N
Newcomb
518.582.4401
Year-round local bar serving
lunch and dinner to residents,
bikers, campers, visitors, and
snowmobilers. Basic food
and drink with prices to
match.
Open daily.

O.P. Frederick's
5064 Route 8
Chestertown
518.494.4141
Warm and inviting
environment. Outdoor seating
overlooking backwater edge
of Loon Lake. Occasional live
music. Imaginative drink and
meal specials.
Closes in December and April.

Eastern Lakes

Barnsider Smokehouse
2112 State Route 9
Lake George
518.668.5268
Family-run barbecue
restaurant. Small service
bar offering a decent
selection of beer, wine, and
liquor. Outdoor deck
seating and occasional
entertainment.
Open year-round.

East Cove
Restaurant & Bar
3873 State Route 9L
Lake George
518.668.5265
Tavern for regulars and
tourists; service bar for
restaurant. Specialty drinks,
pub menu, and full dining.
Warm, rustic interior. Pleasant
staff and patrons.
Open year-round.

Hague Firehouse
9813 Graphite Mt. Road
Hague
518.543.6266
Industrial-chic styling and
sophisticated atmosphere.
Generous wine pours,
interesting drink menu, full

TRAILHEADS

dinner menu. Deck seating. Check website for days and hours.
Open May to October.

JC Montana's
267 Canada Street
Lake George
518.668.5085
Located in center of Lake George village, with patio overlooking Shepard Park. Bar is trendy, with soft elements. Popular with tourists and locals. Specialty margaritas and martinis. Fine dining choices.
Open year-round.

Lakeside Lodge & Grille
4934 Lake Shore Drive
Bolton Landing
518.644.5253
Located in the heart of Bolton Landing. Adirondack décor. Outdoor summer seating in the shade. Bar primarily serves lunch and dinner guests.
Open year-round.

Market Place Steakhouse
4957 Lake Shore Drive
Bolton Landing
518.644.3663
Nice, modern tavern with sports-bar character. Weekly music and open mic night. Cocktails and beer specials at reasonable prices.
Open year-round.

North Country Club
1795 Route 9N
Keeseville
518.834.7730
Somewhat dated décor has charm. Specialty drinks, wines, good beer variety, complimentary hors d'oeuvres. Gourmet pizzas. Kindly patrons and staff.
Open year-round.

Olde Log Inn
2814 Route 9
Lake George
518.668.3334
Local pub north of Lake George Village. Country log interior and exterior. Outdoor deck seating and sufficient room at the bar. Always ready for newcomers.
Open year-round.

The Pub
105 Montcalm Street
Ticonderoga
518.585.7575
Fairly new décor with lots of

wood. Large, native-American chainsaw carving at entrance. Average sized with wraparound bar. Pub food, occasional live music, beer and wings specials. Open year-round.

Rick's Restaurant & Pub
3922 NYS Route 22
Willsboro
518.963.4371
A diner with a bar in it. Serves draft and bottled beers, wine, and a few pre-packaged specialty drinks. After-work type of local bar. Food options cover a wide range including homemade desserts.
Open year-round.

Shepard's Cove
3 Lower Montcalm Street
Lake George
518.668.4988
A great summer atmosphere in the village. Large bar overlooks Lake George. Interior transitions to deck. Frequent live solo entertainment. Full range of beer and specialty drinks.
Closed in winter.

Stone Manor Restaurant
4436 Lake Shore Drive
Bolton Landing
518.644.5400
At Blue Water Manor, down by the lake. Extensive menu, drink specialties, terrific staff, frequent live music. Seating at the bar with a view, or on the deck with a better view. Magnificent stone fireplace. A must see.
Open May to October.

Upper Deck at Willsboro Bay
25 Klein Way
Willsboro
518.963.8271
Nice summer atmosphere with open-air, "garage-door" windows overlooking the lake. Great views from the deck. Numerous drink options. Bar primarily frequented by boaters on Lake Champlain.
Open summer only.

Southern & Sacandaga

Old Trail Inn
232 N. Shore Road
Hadley
518.863.6419
Welcoming country bar and restaurant. Pleasant staff and affable patrons. Serving drinks, lunch, and dinner at reasonable prices.
Open year-round.

Trailheads

Tavern 16
16 Warrensburg Road
Stony Creek
518.696.5949
A must see mini-museum in the center of Stony Creek. Small bar with a lot of character, frequented by a lot of characters. Quality bartenders. Food is occasionally served for neighborhood parties. Open year-round.

Timeless Tavern & Inn
162 South Main Street
Northville
518.863.4635
Bar and restaurant with a decent menu. Oversized bar. Lots of pine finishes. Comfortable, homey atmosphere. Six rooms available.
Open year-round.

Waterhouse Restaurant
85 Lake Avenue
Lake Luzerne
518.696.3115
A friendly neighborhood bar and restaurant where regulars gather to fraternize with tourists. Nice outdoor seating area. Occasional open mic nights. Able bartenders serve the bar and restaurant. Open year-round.

High Peaks

20 Main Bar
14231 State Route 9N
Au Sable Forks
518.647.8812
It's the only bar in town. Drinks are simple. No food is served. Friendly hometown bar with frequent musical entertainment. Open daily.

Belvedere Restaurant
102 Bloomingdale Avenue
Saranac Lake
518.891.9873
Quaint, family-run Italian restaurant with bar. Nostalgic décor, staff, and patrons. Great place for just a drink, if you can resist the tempting smells from the restaurant. Cash only.
Call for days and times open.

The Cowboy
2226 Saranac Avenue
Lake Placid
518.837.5069
Unique environment. Limited seating at the bar, but tavern

and outdoor seating supplement. Creativity behind the bar adds distinction. Serves breakfast, lunch, and dinner.
Call or check website for hours.

Dancing Bears
2404 Main Street
Lake Placid
518.523.3619
Popular tourist venue with the coldest beer in town, indoor or outdoor seating, and full dining options.
Open daily.

Deer's Head Inn
7552 Court Street
Elizabethtown
518.873.6514
Charming, upscale Adirondack inn. Cozy tavern with excellent service, creative drink menu, and a sociable atmosphere.
Hours and days vary with season.
Check website or call.

Desperado's
2090 Saranac Avenue
Lake Placid
518.523.1507
Tequila—170 different types of tequila! Most interesting beer list. Dos Equis, Tecate, Modelo, Lagunitas. Extensive margarita and drink menu. Mexican restaurant with an Irish twist.
Open year-round.

Great Adirondack Steak & Seafood
2442 Main Street
Lake Placid
518.523.1629
Small, sophisticated Adirondack tavern for restaurant and bar clientele. Serving wine, liquor, and their own Great Adirondack Brewery beer. Growlers to go. Outdoor seating and occasional music on patio.
Open year-round.

Northwoods Inn
2520 Main Street
Lake Placid
518.523.1818
Two bars and a full-service restaurant located in the center of downtown Lake Placid. Spacious and recently renovated. Occasional music. Some drink specials. Open for lunch and dinner.
Open year-round.

Trailheads

Straight Shot Lounge at the Golden Arrow Resort
2543 Main Street
Lake Placid
518.837.5052
Bright, contemporary décor with adjoining restaurant. Great Happy Hour specials.
Open daily, year-round.

Tail O' the Pup
1152 Route 86
Ray Brook
518.572.9000
A classic roadside attraction. Indoor and outdoor bar with live music, frozen margaritas, and picnic barbecue. Cabins for rent on the premises. Arcade, camp store, ice cream, lobster shack.
Open May to October.

The Waterhole
48 Main Street
Saranac Lake
518.891.9502
A biker bar with an interesting stone motif. Regulars share the Waterhole with anyone who stops in. Limited drink choices. Small outdoor seating area. Music venue on weekend nights.
Open year-round.

Western Wilderness

Cranberry Lake Lodge
7202 State Highway 3
Cranberry Lake
315.848.3301
Direct access from the lake or roadside. Restaurant and tavern have old-time lodge appeal. Enjoy casual lakeside drinks in the summer or warm up at the bar in the winter.
Open year-round.

Drake's Inn
363 Route 28
Inlet
315.357.5181
Mom-and-Pop bar and small, busy restaurant. Local-retiree and seasonal-resident population in a cozy, timeless atmosphere.
Open year-round.

Glenmore Bar & Grill
146 Glenmore Road
Eagle Bay
315.357.4891
Reputedly haunted historic hotel with nice views of Big Moose

Lake from the bar and deck. Sprawling ranch atmosphere. Unique drink specials. Popular spot for snowmobilers. Food and drink at reasonable prices. Open year-round.

Ole Barn
74 Limekiln Lake Road
Inlet
315.357.4000
Spacious, open bar area with surrounding booths and a separate dining room. Great for large parties. Large liquor selection. Beer served in cans only. Home of the "beer can express." Closed briefly in fall and spring.

Red Dog Tavern
2682 South Shore Road
Inlet
315.357.5502
Primarily a restaurant. Notorious for extra-hot "Armageddon" wings. Small bar has Irish influence. Specialty martinis. Seasonal regulars create a local pub atmosphere. Closed briefly in November and April.

Slickers
3132 State Route 28
Old Forge
315.369.3002
Bar and restaurant. Bar is small and can easily get crowded. Music is featured on weekends.

Nice lake view and deck area. Drinks are fairly standard. Open year-round.

Trails End
41 Raquette River Drive
Tupper Lake
518.359.7135
Biker bar with friendly clientele. Beer is the signature drink, but bar is stocked with the basics. Frequent music venue. Nice view from the porch. No food is served here. Open daily, year-round.

Van Auken's Inne
108 Forge Street
Thendara
315.369.3033
A very old inn, with a somewhat updated bar. Hearty tavern menu and drinks. A casual atmosphere, frequented by inn guests and seasonal visitors. Open year-round.

Wayback Inn
1910 Big Moose Road
Eagle Bay
315.357.6000
Recently renovated bar and restaurant. Secluded location beyond Big Moose Lake, with large outdoor area conducive to biker and snowmobile parties. Rooms for rent. Fun place with creative bar staff. Closed April.

Happy Hour at Home

When we weren't out reviewing bars, we worked diligently in the lab at Pammy's At-Her-on-Deck Pub, creating and taste-testing Adirondack-themed cocktails. Careful analysis and frequent tastings enabled us to separate the good from the bad. Invitations to sampling conferences were much sought after among our friends and acquaintances, who were only too eager to be of assistance.

No people or animals were harmed in the testing of these drinks.

Happy Hour Cocktail Recipes

46er
Adirondack Mudslide
AdironJack Sunrise
Bee Sting
Black Fly Bite
Bloody Oscar
Blue Line Martini
Boreas Pond
Champlain Cocktail
Essex Escape
Forty-Six Peaks
   Pumpkin Martini
Hurricane Irene

Log Jam
Mount Marcy Mimosa
Pitchoff Wallbanger
Polar Plunge
Rhubarb Margarita
Rondeau's Breakfast
Sagamore Sling
Sally Miller Smith
Slippery Nippletop
Ti One On
Tupper Upper
Water-Lily
Whitewater Rushin'

The Recipes

Each of our High Peaks bars was invited to submit a signature drink for the recipe section. You'll find an interesting mix of bloody marys, martinis, margaritas, and other unique concoctions in the Signature Recipes section. Whether you prepare them at home or order one at a High Peaks location, you're sure to enjoy these tasty beverages.

For your safety, each was tested by our independent laboratory.

High Peaks Signature Cocktail Recipes

Adirondack Pub Punch
Basil & Wick's Jeannie 'Rita
Baxter's Tavern Bloody Mary
Big Moose Adirondack Martini
Captain Cook's Roofie Coolata
Charlie's Inn Ecstasy Martini
Cobble Hill Inn Long Island Peach
The Cottage Maple Martini
Duffy's Bloody Mary
Essex Inn's Sinnfully Essex
Friends Lake Inn's L'Orange Martini
Indian Lake Tavern's Apple-Ginger Martini
Inn at Speculator's Adirondack Citrus Cooler
Johnny's Mountain Melon Ball
Lisa G's Grapefruit Cooler
Pub on 9's 9-Tini
Sport Island Pub's Sand Island Breeze
Thirsty Moose Washington Apple
TR's Bully for Watermelons!
Windfall Punch
Witherbee's Amanda's Snickers Martini

46er

A 46-ounce punch to celebrate conquering the 46 High Peaks—be they mountains or taverns. This accomplishment calls for something special: cognac and champagne. Vary fruits and berries according to preference and season and invite several friends to toast your success.

16 oz. champagne (brut is best)
5 oz. Remy Martin cognac
5 oz. pear vodka
5 oz. orange juice
5 oz. cranberry juice
10 oz. strawberry puree
Strawberries, washed and cut
Apple slices
Pears soaked in cognac
Mix all ingredients in large punch bowl with ice. Add fresh strawberries, apples, and the cognac-soaked pears. Serve in a punch glass or champagne flute. Garnish with berries.

Serving for two

3 oz. champagne
1 oz. Remy Martin cognac
1 oz. pear vodka
1 oz. orange juice
1 oz. cranberry juice
2 oz. strawberry puree
Mix all ingredients except champagne in shaker with ice. Strain into a champagne flute and top with champagne. Garnish with berries.

Adirondack Mudslide

The drink that started it all. What do you get when you combine two adventurers and their eye-rolling daughters, a simple question about a drink and the Internet, and a 900-mile car ride? Why, *Happy Hour in the High Peaks*, of course!

1½ oz. 46 Peaks vodka
1½ oz. Kahlua (coffee liqueur)
1 oz. Frangelico (hazelnut liqueur)
1 oz. irish cream
½ c. chocolate peanut butter ice cream
1 c. ice cubes

Mix in blender. Pour into a brandy balloon and drizzle with chocolate syrup.

AdironJack Sunrise

Despite our father's claim that JD should only be consumed straight up, we couldn't resist messing with it.

1 oz. Jack Daniel's Honey
1 oz. Jack Daniel's whiskey
4 oz. orange juice
½ oz. grenadine

Shake with ice and pour over ice into large rocks glass. Add grenadine and garnish with an orange wheel.

Bee Sting

A little bite with a sweet, gentle buzz.

1 oz. Jack Daniel's Honey
1 oz. triple sec
1 oz. lemon juice
½ tsp. honey
1 oz. water

Shake with ice and strain into a liqueur glass. Garnish with a lemon slice.

Black Fly Bite

If you've spent any time in the Adirondacks, you know all about the black fly.

½ oz. grenadine
½ oz. cherry brandy
1 oz. black sambuca

Slowly pour each ingredient, in the above order, over a bar spoon into a shot glass.

Happy Hour

Bloody Oscar

Our version of the bloody mary, named after Oscar's Smokehouse in Warrensburg, and one of the best uses of Bakon vodka.

1 oz. Bakon vodka
1 oz. 46 Peaks vodka
6 oz. tomato juice
1 tsp. horseradish
1 tsp. lemon juice
1 dash tabasco
1 dash black pepper
1 pinch red pepper flakes
Shake with ice and pour into a highball glass or goblet.
Garnish with celery, tomato, and your favorite tidbits from Oscar's Smokehouse.

Blue Line Martini

A simple blend of regional flavors found "inside the Blue Line."

3 oz. Tangueray gin
1 oz. sweet vermouth
¼ c. pureed blueberries
1 T sugar (optional)
Shake with ice and strain into a chilled cocktail glass. Garnish with a lemon slice.
Variances (allowed): A squeeze of fresh lemon complements and enhances the blueberry flavor. Or, for a sweeter martini, add I oz. Limoncello (lemon liqueur).

Cocktail Recipes

Champlain Cocktail

A potent mixture in homage to the French explorer.
2 oz. Crown Royal
1 oz. Grand Marnier
Pour over ice into a rocks glass. Garnish with an orange wedge.

Boreas Pond

Named after the ponds located in the High Peaks Region of the Adirondack Park. This is best made by the pitcher. You're going to want more!
2 oz. Midori (melon liqueur)
1 oz. triple sec
1 oz. melon vodka
1 pkg. sour mix
1 lemon wedge, squeezed
2 oz. water
Shake with ice and pour into a highball glass. Garnish with melon balls and a lemon slice.

Essex Escape

This drink was created on a beautiful summer day at the Old Dock House.
1 oz. mango vodka
1 oz. coconut rum
3 oz. pineapple juice
Stir and serve over ice in a highball glass. Garnish with a pineapple wedge.

Forty-Six Peaks
Pumpkin Martini

Inspired by a featured drink special served at our very first bar review—Trapper's Tavern at the Copperfield Inn.

1 oz. 46 Peaks vodka
1 oz. Pinnacle Whipped vodka
1 oz. Sapling (maple liqueur)
2 oz. light cream or milk
2 T pumpkin puree
Combine in a blender or shake well with ice. Strain into a martini glass rimmed with coarse sugar and cinnamon. Top with whipped cream. Lightly dust with nutmeg. Garnish with a cinnamon stick.

Hurricane Irene

You have to do something while "hunkered down" in the storm. This recipe makes two servings because you shouldn't be alone in a storm.
3 oz. passion fruit liqueur (two brands are Hpnotiq or Alize)
2 oz. peach schnapps
1½ oz. white rum
1½ oz. dark rum
4 oz. grapefruit juice
Shake with ice and serve in (you guessed it) a hurricane glass!

Log Jam

Logs were once transported through the Adirondacks via riverways, at great peril. This drink is in tribute to those who perished.

1 oz. Wild Turkey bourbon
1 oz. Smirnoff cranberry vodka
1 oz. 46 Peaks vodka
2 oz. cranberry juice
Ginger ale

Shake all ingredients except ginger ale. Pour over ice in a highball glass and top with ginger ale. Garnish with leaf of fresh thyme (if you have the thyme).

Mount Marcy Mimosa

The highest peak in the Adirondacks warrants champagne. The addition of black currant liqueur is inspired by Teddy Roosevelt, who is rumored to have been on Mount Marcy when he received word that McKinley had been shot, and is presumed to have liked currants.

1 oz. crème de cassis (black currant liqueur)
2 dashes Grand Marnier
Champagne
2 oz. orange juice

Stir and serve in a champagne flute.

Pitchoff Wallbanger

For the numerous trips past Pitchoff Wall, on our way to Lake Placid.

1 oz. dark rum
½ oz. Grand Marnier
3 oz. orange juice
½ oz. Galliano

Stir rum, Grand Marnier, and orange juice in a highball glass with ice. Float Galliano on top. Garnish with an orange wedge.

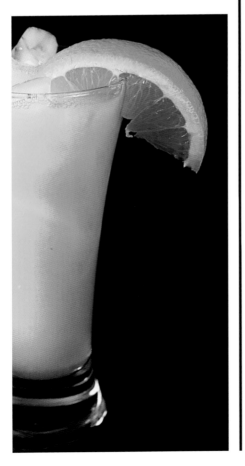

Polar Plunge

An annual ritual in Lake George, this is our contribution to the event. A very refreshing drink in winter or summer.

1½ oz. light rum
½ oz. triple sec
Dash of blue curaçao
1 packet sour mix (or juice of
   1 lemon and 1 tsp. superfine
   sugar)
2 oz. water
8 cubes of ice, crushed

Pour all ingredients into a shaker with ice. Shake and strain into a large rocks glass filled with crushed ice.

Rhubarb Margarita

What else are we supposed to do with our annual crop of rhubarb?

2 oz. tequila
½ oz. triple sec
½ c. cooked rhubarb
½ c. rhubarb syrup
Juice of ½ fresh lime
Blend with ice and serve in a salt-rimmed margarita glass. Garnish with a slice of lime.

Rondeau's Breakfast

We don't know if Adirondack hermit Noah John Rondeau drank, but breakfast is the most important meal.

1 oz. Sapling (maple liqueur)
1 oz. Bakon vodka
½ oz. coffee brandy
2 oz. cranberry juice
Pour all ingredients into a shaker with ice. Shake and strain into a martini glass.

Cocktail Recipes

Sagamore Sling

Named after the Sagamore Hotel in Bolton Landing, this drink is as busy as the hotel in July.

2 oz. gin
¾ oz. Chambord (raspberry liqueur)
½ oz. Jagermeister
½ oz. Cointreau (orange liqueur)
2 oz. pineapple juice
¾ oz. lime juice
2 dashes pomegranate juice
Dash of grenadine
Dash of Angostura bitters

Shake with ice and strain into a tulip glass or a hurricane glass. Garnish with a maraschino cherry, a pineapple wedge, and an orange wheel.

Sally Miller Smith

Like its namesake, this cocktail is gutsy and strong, though more palatable than Prohibition-era bootleg booze. A devout drinker, Sally bought out inventories of three liquor stores just as Prohibition went into effect and stashed it in hidden closets throughout her Schroon Lake home.

3 oz. Canadian whisky
1 oz. sweet vermouth

Pour into a rocks glass filled with ice and garnish with a cherry.

Variation:

Sally wouldn't have done this, but this isn't the 1930s and we don't quite have her grit:
Add just a splash of orange juice and a dash of cherry juice.

Slippery Nippletop

Named after Nippletop Mountain, an Adirondack High Peak. This is our version of the slippery nipple.
½ oz. white sambuca
½ oz. butterscotch schnapps
½ oz. Bailey's Irish Cream
Pour sambuca into a shot glass and slowly layer the other ingredients, using a bar spoon. Top with whipped cream.

Ti One On

A variation of the Pimm's Royale with a hint of French influence. Inspired by the 1759 British takeover of Fort Carillon (later renamed Fort Ticonderoga) during the French and Indian War.
1 oz. Pimm's No. 1
½ oz. Cointreau
Champagne
Pour into a champagne flute. Garnish with a strawberry.

Tupper Upper

An adaptation of Thirsty Moose Pub & Grub's Tic Tac. The Tupper Upper will keep you ticking just a little bit longer.
1 oz. Three Olives Loopy vodka
3 oz. Red Bull
Chill with ice in a shaker and strain into a cordial glass, tall shooter, or bomber shot glass.

Cocktail Recipes

Water-Lily

The sweet-scented water-lily is a common summer sight in ponds and marshes throughout the Adirondack Park. Though white is the native variety, we couldn't resist naming this light and refreshing cooler after the fragrant floater.

1 oz. Absolut Ruby Red vodka
1 oz. Absolut Citron
2 oz. seltzer
2 oz. ruby red grapefruit juice
Pour ingredients into a highball glass filled with ice. Stir, sip, and float.

Whitewater Rushin'

Springtime brings forth icy rushing waters in the rivers of the Adirondack Park, their rapids at peak. Combine that with the sweet flow of maple sugar season and you have our version of the white russian. Named for the annual Hudson River Whitewater Derby, held on the first weekend in May in the North Creek area, it's no mint julep.

2 oz. Sapling (maple liqueur)
1 oz. vanilla vodka
2 oz. light cream
Mix in a blender with ice and serve in a rocks glass. Drizzle with maple syrup.

High Peaks

Adirondack Pub Punch

2 oz. vodka
1½ oz. peach schnapps
1½ oz. sour apple pucker
Fill with orange juice
Splash of grenadine
Shake and serve in a pint glass with ice. Garnish with an orange slice.

Basil & Wick's Jeannie 'Rita

1½ oz. gold tequila
½ oz. triple sec
Fill remainder of glass with ⅓ sour mix, ⅓ cranberry juice, and ⅓ orange juice.
Shake until frothy and pour into a salted pint glass. Garnish with lemon, lime, and orange wheels.

Big Moose Adirondack Martini

1½ oz. 46 Peaks vodka
½ oz. Kahlua (coffee liqueur)
½ oz. Disaronno amaretto
1 oz. New York State maple
  syrup, stirred into solution
Shake with ice and strain into a chilled martini glass. Top with a cherry.

Baxter's Tavern Bloody Mary

1½ oz. Absolut Citron vodka
4 oz. V-8 juice
1 oz. sour mix
Dash of A-1 steak sauce
Dash of pepper
Horseradish
Serve in a tulip glass with a salted rim. Garnish with lemon and olives.

Captain Cook's Roofie Coolata

1 oz. vanilla vodka
1 oz. raspberry vodka
1 oz. blueberry vodka
1 oz. orange vodka
1 oz. blue curaçao
Shake with ice and top with
2 oz. Sprite
2 oz. lemonade
Serve over ice in a pint glass.
Garnish with an orange slice.

Charlie's Inn Ecstasy Martini

2 oz. Three Olives grape vodka
Splash of blue curaçao
Splash of grenadine
Club soda
Shake all ingredients with ice
except club soda and strain into
a martini glass. Top with club soda
and garnish with an orange slice.

Signature Recipes

Cobble Hill Inn
Long Island Peach

½ jigger white rum
½ jigger vodka
½ jigger tequila
½ jigger gin
½ jigger peach schnapps
⅓ jigger triple sec
1 oz. cola
1 oz. sour mix
Shake vigorously with ice.
Serve in a chilled highball glass.
Garnish with a wedge of lemon.

The Cottage Maple Martini

4 oz. 46 Peaks vodka
1 tsp. local maple syrup
Shake vigorously with ice. Serve
straight up in a martini glass.

Duffy's Bloody Mary

1–2 oz. vodka
8 oz. tomato juice
1 tsp. minced horseradish
1 shake Worcestershire sauce
1 shake tabasco sauce
1 shake pepper
Dash of celery salt
Serve over ice in a pint glass.
Garnish with a celery stalk.

High Peaks

Essex Inn's Sinnfully Essex

2 oz. vodka
2 oz. Chambord (raspberry liqueur)
Splash of cranberry juice
Shake with ice and strain into a martini glass rimmed with red coarse sugar. Garnish with a brandy-soaked cherry.

Friends Lake Inn's L'Orange Martini

2 oz. Grey Goose L'Orange
2 oz. Grand Marnier
Fresh lemon juice
Wild clover honey
Shake with ice and strain into a martini glass. Garnish with an orange peel.

Indian Lake Tavern's Apple-Ginger Martini

1½ oz. Stoli apple vodka
½ oz. ginger brandy
1½ oz. apple juice
Shake with ice and strain into a martini glass rimmed with raw brown sugar.

Inn at Speculator's Adirondack Citrus Cooler

1–2 oz. grapefruit vodka
2 oz. lemonade
2 oz. cranberry juice
Squeeze of fresh lime
Shake with ice and pour into a tall glass with plenty of ice. Garnish with a lemon slice.

Lisa G's Grapefruit Cooler

2 oz. champagne
1 oz. gin
1 oz. St. Germain (elderflower liqueur)
2 oz. grapefruit juice
1 oz. simple syrup
Splash of grenadine
Squirt of fresh lemon juice
Club soda

Shake all ingredients with ice except club soda. Pour into a pint Mason jar. Add a squeeze of an orange slice and top with club soda. Garnish with an orange wedge.

Johnny's Mountain Melon Ball

1½ oz. Captain Morgan Parrot Bay coconut rum
1 oz. melon liqueur
1 oz. pineapple juice

Shake with ice and strain into a martini glass. Garnish with a cherry.

Pub on 9's 9-Tini

The "parts" add up to 9, but we recommend you don't use ounces!

5 parts (2½ oz.) Three Olives
  vodka
2 parts (1 oz.) Three Olives
  grape vodka
2 parts (1 oz.) Three Olives
  cherry vodka

Shake with ice and strain into a martini glass. Garnish with a cherry.

Sport Island Pub's
Sand Island Breeze

1¼ oz. coconut rum
1 oz. banana liqueur
¼ oz. blue curaçao
6 oz. pineapple juice
Serve over ice in a pint glass. Garnish with a cherry.

Thirsty Moose
Washington Apple

1 oz. Crown Royal
1 oz. apple pucker
Splash of cranberry juice
Shake, strain, and serve as shots with friends.

TR's Bully for Watermelons!

1 oz. Smirnoff watermelon vodka
4 oz. cranberry juice
Splash of ginger ale
Serve over ice in a highball glass. Garnish with a watermelon wedge.

Windfall Punch

1 part gin
1 part cranberry juice
1 part Minute Maid lemonade
Prepare in a punch bowl or make as an individual serving. Add lots of ice and serve in your favorite glass. Garnish with a lemon wedge.

Witherbee's Amanda's Snickers Martini

1 oz. Absolut vodka
1 oz. Kahlua (coffee liqueur)
1 oz. Disaronno amaretto
1 oz. Bailey's Irish Cream
1 oz. Frangelico (hazelnut liqueur)
Shake with ice and strain into a martini glass rimmed with chocolate syrup.

High Peaks At-a-Glance

BAR	REGION	LOCATION
Adirondack Hotel Tap Room	Foothills Region	Long Lake
barVino	Foothills Region	North Creek
Basil & Wick's	Foothills Region	North Creek
Friends Lake Inn Wine Bar	Foothills Region	Chestertown
George Henry's	Foothills Region	Warrensburg
Indian Lake Restaurant & Tavern	Foothills Region	Indian Lake
Panther Mountain Pub	Foothills Region	Chestertown
Sporty's Iron Duke Saloon	Foothills Region	Minerva
Trapper's Tavern at Copperfield Inn	Foothills Region	North Creek
Witherbee's Carriage House	Foothills Region	Schroon Lake
Adirondack Bar and Grill	Eastern Lakes Region	Queensbury
Adirondack Pub & Brewery	Eastern Lakes Region	Lake George
The Burleigh House	Eastern Lakes Region	Ticonderoga
Duffy's Tavern	Eastern Lakes Region	Lake George
Essex Inn Tavern	Eastern Lakes Region	Essex
Frederick's Restaurant & Lounge	Eastern Lakes Region	Bolton Landing
Johnny's Smokehouse & Sports Bar	Eastern Lakes Region	Willsboro
Judd's Tavern	Eastern Lakes Region	Lake George
Old Dock House Restaurant & Marina	Eastern Lakes Region	Essex
Pub on 9	Eastern Lakes Region	Bolton
TR's Lounge at the Holiday Inn Resort	Eastern Lakes Region	Lake George
Inn at Speculator	Southern & Sacandaga Region	Speculator
Lake House Grille	Southern & Sacandaga Region	Wells
Long Horn Restaurant & Pub	Southern & Sacandaga Region	Luzerne
Melody Lodge Tap Room	Southern & Sacandaga Region	Speculator
Oxbow Inn	Southern & Sacandaga Region	Piseco
Sport Island Pub	Southern & Sacandaga Region	Northville
Stony Creek Inn	Southern & Sacandaga Region	Stony Creek
Baxter Mountain Tavern	High Peaks Region	Keene
Captain Cook's Bar & Grill	High Peaks Region	Saranac Lake
Charlie's Inn	High Peaks Region	Lake Clear
Cobble Hill Inn	High Peaks Region	Elizabethtown
The Cottage at Mirror Lake Inn	High Peaks Region	Lake Placid
Grizle T's	High Peaks Region	Saranac Lake
Lake Placid Pub & Brewery	High Peaks Region	Lake Placid
Liquids and Solids at the Handlebar	High Peaks Region	Lake Placid
Lisa G's	High Peaks Region	Lake Placid
Zig Zags Pub	High Peaks Region	Lake Placid
Big Moose Inn & Restaurant	Western Wilderness Region	Eagle Bay
Daiker's	Western Wilderness Region	Old Forge
Matt's Draft House at Screamen Eagle	Western Wilderness Region	Inlet
P-2's Irish Pub	Western Wilderness Region	Tupper Lake
Thirsty Moose Pub & Grub	Western Wilderness Region	Childwold
Tony Harper's Too	Western Wilderness Region	Old Forge
TOW Bar Inn	Western Wilderness Region	Old Forge
Windfall Bar & Grill	Western Wilderness Region	Cranberry Lake

Acknowledgments

So many people offered support, answered questions, tested cocktails, and told us where to go. Our sincerest appreciation to the few we're able to mention here:

A thousand thanks to Lawrence P. Gooley and Jill Jones of Bloated Toe Publishing. Larry—editor, publisher, and kind of funny guy—kept us going with words of encouragement and praise, along with many lessons in grammar and punctuation. Known amongst ourselves as the Comma-Kaze, we swore Larry was charging by the comma. Larry gave us the confidence to reach more than a little outside the boundaries. Jill—webmaster, Photoshop guru, all-around techie, and silent partner (though we're sure Larry would disagree)—kept Larry on track. Jill was always right.

Karen Muermann for liking everything we wrote just because we're her daughters.

Jane Peter, who opened Basil & Wick's at about the same time we began our bar reviews, has been a constant promoter of our endeavors and always made us feel like celebrities. Jeannie Russell, Basil & Wick's bartender extraordinaire, for her mixology expertise and all-around sunny disposition.

Bar owners and patrons, who urged us on, shared stories and information, and made our visits memorable.

John Warren for inviting us to contribute to the *Adirondack Almanack*. The weekly *Almanack* deadline kept us on track even when we didn't feel like going to a bar (yes, it happened), or writing about it.

Mohan's Liquor Store, Queensbury. For not giving us the hairy eyeball when we asked for some rather off-the-wall spirits.

We are indebted to our families for their support, though reluctant at times. They tolerated take-out, suffered our neglect, and kept their objections to themselves. Little by little, they came to believe. Even Sydney.

Tina and Acacia, Vermont mules, who ran Sapling across the border for us.

Pammy's At-Her-on-Deck Pub, a private, members-only home bar and storage facility for all those Mohan's purchases.

And finally, to our friends. For believing in us and for always being there when the booze was flowing.

Cover design & map illustrations: Kaleb Ladd-Cocca & Jonathan Haines, Vicious Circle Design, Atlanta, Georgia

Product permissions: Sapling Vermont Maple Liqueur, Brattleboro, Vermont; Lake Placid Spirits, Lake Placid, New York; and Oscar's Smokehouse, Warrensburg, New York—permission to feature their products among our pages

Photography: Lifescapes Photography by Kim Ladd

Logo Design: Kim Ladd

Mixology: Pam Ladd

Glassware: All featured barware courtesy of the Pam Ladd Collection

About the Authors

Kim Ladd and Pam Ladd are sisters and best friends. Together they have more than 70 years' drinking experience. They will neither confirm nor deny the legality of all those years.

Kim's affection for craft beer and Pam's fondness for all things shaken have allowed them to contribute in areas of their own particular interest. Their similarities, differences, individual strengths, and quirky genetics complement one another and have made a collaboration of

Kim (left) and Pam (right) test their recipes in the drink lab at Pammy's At-Her-on-Deck Pub (Photograph by Acacia Ladd-Cocca)

this sort possible. Whether during the interviewing process or the actual writing, Pam's attention to fact and Kim's affinity for fluff created a balance punctuated with their individual and combined senses of humor. Both have lived in the Adirondacks for most of their lives.

Kim and Pam are regular contributors to *Adirondackalmanack.com* and their own blog, *happyhourinthehighpeaks.blogspot.com*. You can follow their further adventures and commentary on Facebook and @ADK46barfly on Twitter.

Pam Ladd has had a lengthy career as a systems analyst and project manager. Her data experience was instrumental in compiling facts about the bars reviewed for this book. Pam enjoys practicing mixology at home, collecting glassware, and exploring the world one bar at a time. She lives in the Foothills Region with her husband and daughter.

Kim Ladd is a freelance photographer specializing in sports, environmental portraiture, and, more recently, cocktail photography. She has a background in visual communications and contributed much of the design and layout for this book. Kim lives with her husband and daughter in Thurman in the Foothills Region of the Adirondack Park.

Both look forward to new opportunities to explore all facets of drinking in exotic locations. Their next project is already under way.

Visit happyhourinthehighpeaks.com for books and other goodies.

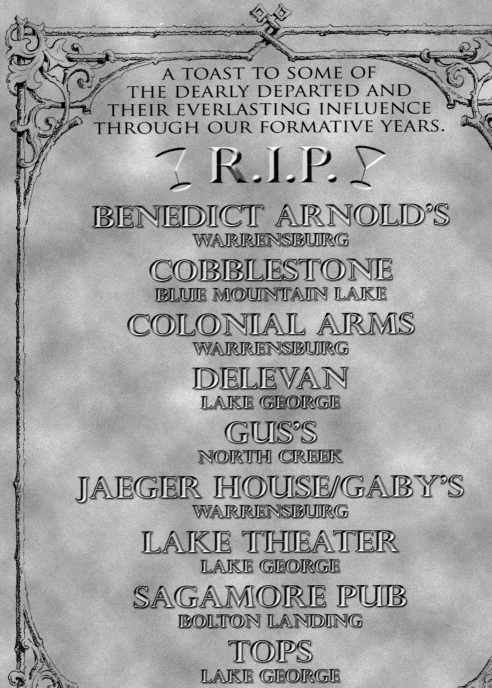

A TOAST TO SOME OF
THE DEARLY DEPARTED AND
THEIR EVERLASTING INFLUENCE
THROUGH OUR FORMATIVE YEARS.

R.I.P.

BENEDICT ARNOLD'S
WARRENSBURG

COBBLESTONE
BLUE MOUNTAIN LAKE

COLONIAL ARMS
WARRENSBURG

DELEVAN
LAKE GEORGE

GUS'S
NORTH CREEK

JAEGER HOUSE/GABY'S
WARRENSBURG

LAKE THEATER
LAKE GEORGE

SAGAMORE PUB
BOLTON LANDING

TOPS
LAKE GEORGE

WELLS HOUSE
POTTERSVILLE